CAMBRIDGE TEXTS AND STUDIES IN
THE HISTORY OF EDUCATION

General Editors
A. C. F. BEALES, A. V. JUDGES, J. P. C. ROACH

EDUCATION AND THE FRENCH
REVOLUTION

IN THIS SERIES

Texts

Fénelon on Education, edited by H. C. Barnard
Friedrich Froebel, a selection edited by Irene Lilley
Matthew Arnold and the Education of the New Order,
edited by Peter Smith and Geoffrey Summerfield
(*in preparation*)
Robert Owen on Education, edited by Harold Silver
(*in preparation*)
James Mill on Education, edited by W. H. Burston
(*in preparation*)

Studies

Education and the French Revolution, by H. C. Barnard

OTHER VOLUMES IN PREPARATION

EDUCATION AND
THE FRENCH REVOLUTION

BY

H. C. BARNARD

Emeritus Professor of Education
University of Reading

CAMBRIDGE

AT THE UNIVERSITY PRESS

1969

CAMBRIDGE UNIVERSITY PRESS
Cambridge, New York, Melbourne, Madrid, Cape Town, Singapore,
São Paulo, Delhi

Cambridge University Press
The Edinburgh Building, Cambridge CB2 8RU, UK

Published in the United States of America by
Cambridge University Press, New York

www.cambridge.org
Information on this title: www.cambridge.org/9780521108881

First published 1969
This digitally printed version 2009

A catalogue record for this publication is available from the British Library

Library of Congress Catalogue Card Number: 68-23174

ISBN 978-0-521-07256-4 hardback
ISBN 978-0-521-10888-1 paperback

Contents

Preface

In the preface to *The French Tradition in Education*, which was published by the Cambridge University Press in 1922, I said 'The period of the Revolution I have left untouched because the educational activities which are associated with it seem to me of so great importance that they would merit a separate treatise consecrated solely to this subject'. I had hoped some day to try to fill this lacuna; but other commitments have always prevented this, although over the years I have been collecting material and doing some work on the subject as and when I could. However, owing largely to the encouragement and help of Professor A. V. Judges, I have at last been given an opportunity to make the attempt; and I should like to express to him my sincere gratitude.

To do full justice to this theme would entail the labour of a lifetime, and the result would be in every sense a *magnum opus*. What I have tried to do therefore is to present an essential outline which may, I hope, prove of some value and interest to the student or the non-specialist reader.

I am much indebted to Professor Vernon Mallinson, who most kindly read through my MS. and made some helpful suggestions; and also to Mr G. W. Geoghegan and Mr G. G. Hatton, of the Reading University Institute of Education library, who afforded me willing and expert professional assistance.

PREFACE

The Bibliographical Appendix is to some extent based on an article which I contributed to the *British Journal of Educational Studies* of November 1965. I should like to thank the editor, Professor A. C. F. Beales, for kindly allowing me to make use of it.

H.C.B.

1 *French education in the period immediately preceding the Revolution*

In order to assess the effect of the French Revolution in the field of education—what it did, what it proposed to do, what it failed to do—it is necessary first to examine the educational provision that was available in the country before the Revolution occurred. It is certainly not true that under the *Ancien Régime* France lacked educational facilities; in this respect she was probably in a better position than any other European country. But although schools of various kinds, colleges, technical institutions and universities existed, they were on the whole in need of reform and badly distributed and their mutual relationships were ill-organised. Also they were in almost every case directly or indirectly under the control or supervision of the Church. This is not to say that the State had never shown any concern about educational matters. For example, the reform of the University of Paris in 1600 had been due to 'L'ordre et la volonté du très-chrétien et très invincible roi de France et de Navarre, Henri IV', and not to any ecclesiastical authority. Again, after the Revocation of the Edict of Nantes (1685) Louis XIV issued a series of edicts and declarations designed to reinforce its implications. In 1698 a decree was issued that children from the age of seven were to be compelled to attend Catholic schools up to the age of fourteen. But as the necessary elementary schools were lacking in many areas a further *ordonnance* decreed that 'as soon as possible schoolmasters and schoolmistresses shall be appointed in parishes where there are none, in order to instruct children of both sexes in the mysteries of the Catholic Apostolic Roman religion, and also in reading and writing (for those who will need this).'[1] The cost of providing schools and of paying teachers was laid on the inhabitants of the area concerned, and the whole system was put under the supervision of *intendants*, as representing the central authority. But there were no State grants to implement these decrees, and it proved extremely difficult to raise any kind of local education rate. However, the enactment of 1698 was re-affirmed in a *Déclaration du Roi* which dates from 1724. It was equally ineffective. It can therefore be said that prior to the Revolution the intervention of the State in the field of education had been more apparent than real. Although such intervention was, like the Revolution itself, really a political move, it was ostensibly undertaken in defence of the Catholic religion; and it remains true that, such as it was, the educational system of France remained almost entirely under the control of the Church.

Elementary education at the end of the *Ancien Régime* was organised in several different ways. In the cities and larger towns the 'little schools', some for boys and some for girls, were run by masters and mistresses who had to hold a licence, renewable annually and issued by an official called the 'scholaster' (*écolâtre*), who acted as the representative of the bishop. These schools could take children as young as seven, who were taught to read. The custom of teaching the elements of reading by the use of Latin words—usually from the *Salve Regina* or the Penitential Psalms—was by this time gradually being given up. When sufficiently proficient

---

[1] A. Duruy, *L'Instruction publique et la Révolution* (Paris, 1882), p. 5.

in this art, the pupils were advanced to writing and elementary arithmetic—often with the use of counters (*jetons*). The elder children, aged nine to eleven, might even begin Latin; and there was of course at every stage considerable emphasis on religious instruction and practices. The teaching was given individually to each child in turn, while the rest were following in silence or learning something by heart. The simultaneous method of class-teaching was not yet used in this type of school. In the girls' schools needlework took the place of Latin. In order to finance these 'little schools' the licensed masters and mistresses were entitled to charge fees which seem to have varied from place to place or according to the position of the pupil in the school; but there was usually a clause in the scholaster's licence to the effect that the children of very poor parents were to be educated free. In some districts no school-fees were exacted from anyone, especially where the school had been endowed by a founder and not provided by the inhabitants of a parish.

In country areas the control exerted by the scholaster over 'little schools' was less direct. The appointment of the schoolmaster or schoolmistress was usually made by a committee of the local inhabitants, convened and presided over by the *curé*; or it might be made by the local *seigneur* if he had founded and supported the school. But in either case the selected candidate was still required to apply to the scholaster, or other episcopal deputy, for the necessary licence (*lettres de régence*), though this requirement seems sometimes to have been evaded. It is interesting to note that the State, in the person of the *intendant*, had also to confirm the appointment, but only in order to see that the terms of the contract between the teacher and his employers were

1-2

being observed. He did not oppose or rival the Church's authority; but in the long run his position in this respect contributed to the secularisation and centralisation of education during the Revolution.

Owing to their poor salary and low status many of the teachers in the 'little schools' were ignorant and incapable; but sweeping statements about them are not justifiable. In some cases—e.g. at Paris—the standard seems to have been fairly rigorous, and everywhere, as has been said, the *maître* or *maîtresse d'école* had to be licensed by the bishop through his scholaster. It was mainly in the country districts that, owing to lack of suitable candidates, the licence might be given to 'eating-house keepers, to hairdressers and to showmen'. The country schoolmaster often acted also as sacristan or sexton; but in many cases—and this is especially true of the girls' schools—the school might be handed over to a teaching congregation and staffed by members of it. The root of the difficulty, as regards lay teachers, was that there were no facilities for teacher-training, and perhaps a belated realisation of this explains the interest in normal schools shown in the educational programmes of the Revolution period. But even after the Revocation of the Edict of Nantes a certain ecclesiastic named De Chennevières had submitted a memoir[1] to Louis XIV in which he referred to 'L'incomparable nécessité d'establir un séminaire de maistres et un de maistresses d'escole en chaque diocèse'.

Mention should be made of a type of elementary school which was found in Paris and some of the other large towns in France. This is the writing school maintained by members of the Guild of Scriveners,

[1] The original of this document is in the Bibliothèque Nationale, and its date is 1686.

4

whose corporation had been authorised as far back as 1570. Their prime concern was with transcribing legal documents and giving advice in cases of suspected forgery; but they were also allowed to teach writing, spelling and simple arithmetic. Thus their work not only supplemented, but also tended to compete with, that of the official 'little schools'; and there was continual friction between the two types of institution.

The 'little schools' licensed by the scholaster, and the writing schools of the Scriveners' Corporation, were not of themselves sufficient to provide a complete system of elementary education. In many parishes therefore the local *curé* supplied the deficiency by starting an elementary school in which the teaching was often done either by himself or by his curate (*vicaire*). These charity schools were quite free and little was taught in them beyond reading and religious instruction. They were under the control not of the scholaster, but of the *curé* himself, though they might be inspected from time to time by the rural dean. These schools were founded and maintained by funds raised by the Church —parish collections, gifts and bequests; and encouragement was given to possible benefactors. In four successive Assemblies of the French clergy (1750, 1755, 1760 and 1765) the necessity for founding parish schools is stressed. Where this was not possible parishes sometimes maintained Sunday schools (*écoles dominicales*) which simply taught the catechism and the bare elements of reading. Their existence shows that they catered for those who had received no education in a 'little school' or a charity school or elsewhere.

Charity schools were sometimes maintained not by parishes, but by private individuals or by religious orders. The Ursulines, for example, had three hundred houses in France in the second half of the eighteenth century; and the Congregation of Notre Dame, founded by St Pierre Fourier, was also conspicuous for its work in this field. It was estimated by Taine[1] that in 1790 there were in France about 37,000 nuns, a considerable number of whom belonged to various teaching orders. But the most conspicuous of all these congregations was the Institute of the Brothers of the Christian Schools, which had been founded by St Jean-Baptiste De La Salle in 1684. It had made great contributions to education in France—for example, in technical education and in the training of its members; but its chief importance was in the field of free popular education for boys. Although the De La Salle schools had to face competition and opposition from the 'little schools' and the writing masters, by the year 1790 there were 125 of them in various parts of France, with some 1000 teaching brothers and 36,000 pupils. The Institute also made some important contributions to the techniques of elementary instruction. For the 'individual' method, to which reference has been made, De La Salle substituted the 'simultaneous' or class method of teaching. Moreover, instruction in reading was from the beginning related to French, and not to Latin, words. De La Salle also introduced a type of 'higher primary school' in which the curriculum was extended to include mathematics, modern languages, drawing and book-keeping. In all types of educational institution run by the Christian Brothers tuition was free.

To sum up, then, we can say that the provision of elementary education in the period immediately preceding the Revolution was by no means lacking, but it

[1] See *Les Origines de la France contemporaine* (6 vols, Paris, 1876–94), I, chap. ii.

was very badly distributed. The Abbé Allain has discussed this matter in some detail and the statistician Maggiolo has investigated the percentage of illiterates, as indicated by the number of those who were able to sign their marriage registers during the years 1789–90. The north of France seems to have been comparatively well provided with elementary education. In Paris, for example, there were 334 'little schools' (167 of them for girls), as well as writing schools and parish charity schools. In the diocese of Rouen there were only fifteen communes out of 102 which did not possess an elementary school. In Artois an inquiry made in 1790 showed that nearly every village had a *maître d'école* and often a mistress as well. At Rheims there were boys' schools in nearly all the parishes; and this was true even in the country parishes of Alsace, Lorraine, Franche Comté, Côte d'Or and Auxerre. In some rural areas, however, it was customary to run the school only from All Saints' Day to the end of May, so that the children could be free to work on the land during the summer. On the other hand many parts of France were very badly off for elementary schools; and this was especially true of the thinly populated central and western districts—e.g. Périgord, Saintonge, Gironde, Limousin, Auvergne, Brittany. From generalities like this, however, it is difficult to get a clear idea of the actual value and content of the elementary education given in various parts of France in 1789, and here possibly Maggiolo's statistics[1] may be of some value. It is noteworthy, but natural, that the areas where the percentage of literacy is lowest almost always coincide with those least provided

---

[1] Maggiolo's statistics are illustrated by two very interesting maps in M. Gontard, *L'Enseignement primaire en France, 1789–1833* (Paris, n.d.), pp. 17 and 25.

with primary schools. In the Franche Comté, for example, 78·85 per cent of the men and 29·12 per cent of the women were sufficiently literate to sign the marriage register; but in Guyenne, between the Garonne and the Dordogne, the percentages were only 12·4 for men and 7·7 for women. During the years 1786 to 1790 in the whole of France, including the big towns, 47·45 per cent of the bridegrooms and 26·28 per cent of the brides were able to sign their names. At the same time it may perhaps be questioned how far ability to sign one's name is a real test of literacy. In some schools—especially those for girls—the pupils were not taught to write at all. We even read of a *maîtresse d'école* who objected to teaching girls to write lest they might be enabled to send notes to young men. Quite apart from statistics, it is clear that the general standards of teaching, the character and qualifications of the lay teachers, the premises and equipment and hygiene of the schools in many cases left much to be desired. The best elementary schools obviously tended to be the *petites écoles* in the cities and big towns, and also those run by members of religious orders who had been dedicated to, and trained for, the work of teaching.

Secondary education under the *Ancien Régime* was provided in the *collèges* of the teaching congregations and of the Arts faculties of the universities. These ran a course[1] for boys who had already learnt to read and

---

[1] It lasted normally for six years, followed by another two years of 'philosophy'. It was arranged as follows (read from the bottom upwards):

Physicien ⎫ Philosophy Logicien ⎭	Iième (Rhetoric)	IVième (2nd grammar)
	IIième (Humanity)	Vième
	IIIième (1st grammar)	VIième

See for example, Bouquier, *Collège d'Harcourt et Lycée Saint-Louis* (Paris, 1891), pp. 191 ff.

write and had acquired a smattering of arithmetic and elementary Latin in a 'little school' or elsewhere. It has been estimated that on the eve of the Revolution there were 562 *collèges* of various kinds in the country, and that they contained 72,747 pupils of whom about 40,000 held 'free places' (*bourses*). To this we can add a number of *petits séminaires*. These took pupils from the age of twelve who were designed for the priesthood and who would be transferred at the age of seventeen or eighteen to a *grand séminaire*—a specialised theological college. For girls secondary education was provided in convent schools—most of them boarding establishments—run, like many of the elementary schools, by teaching orders of women.[1] The age of the pupils would be from about ten to eighteen. In the boys' *collèges* the staple of the curriculum was Latin and Greek, though some of the teaching orders also provided instruction in such subjects as mathematics and history; and the teaching of Greek in some of the Faculty of Arts colleges was said to be unsatisfactory.[2] In all types of school alike religious instruction and observances bulked largely.

Of the teaching congregations concerned with secondary education by far the most important was the Society of Jesus which had started work in France in 1565. It rapidly extended its influence and some of the most prominent Frenchmen of the seventeenth and eighteenth centuries—e.g. Descartes and Voltaire— were educated in Jesuit schools. It was even said that 'nobody who reasoned against the Jesuits but owed it to the Jesuits that he was able to reason at all'. But the

[1] See H. C. Barnard, *Girls at School under the Ancien Régime*, (London, 1954), pp. 36–49.
[2] Cf. 'Jamais le proverbe ancien *Graecum est, non legitur* ne reçut une application plus juste qu'aujourd'hui' (Philipon de la Madelaine, *De l'éducation des Collèges*, Paris, 1784, p. 127).

Society remained ultramontane in outlook, and in spite of its educational efficiency it incurred a rising tide of criticism, and this resulted in the expulsion of the order from France. Its dissolution was pronounced by the Parlement de Paris[1] in 1762, and this was confirmed by royal edict in 1764. At this time there were no less than eighty-six Jesuit colleges, grouped in five different provinces, in the whole of France. The expulsion of the order involved the closing down of these schools, and this meant a most serious loss to the provision of secondary education. Various attempts were made to fill this gap. The Parlement de Paris sent four of its members to the chief universities of France in order to collect information and report on possible schemes. It was suggested that the colleges vacated by the Jesuits might be brought under the jurisdiction of local universities; but difficulties of staffing and organisation, as well as disputes and jealousies, prevented action being taken. At Paris, however, some of the smaller colleges of the university, which were languishing and had few students, were amalgamated with the College of Louis-le-Grand, which had been the chief Jesuit school in the metropolis. It was hoped that the re-organised institution might prove 'une pépinière abondante de maîtres dont l'État a besoin et qui répandront partout l'éducation'—a scheme for training teachers which was abortively developed thirty-one years later during the Revolution.[2] In some provincial

[1] The *parlements* were supreme law courts. They also had the right of 'registering' royal edicts, and of 'remonstrating' if there was anything with which they disagreed. In 1789 there were in all thirteen *parlements* in France, but the area of jurisdiction of the Parlement de Paris was by far the largest and covered nearly one-third of the whole country. Refer to the map in Cobban, *History of Modern France* (2 vols, London, 1962), I, 67.

[2] See below, pp. 152-5.

towns an ex-Jesuit college was taken over by a secular municipal authority; but even so many of the staff would probably be ecclesiastics. It was more usual to transfer such schools to one of the existing teaching orders—in particular the Oratorians, Benedictines, Doctrinaires and Barnabites.

Perhaps the most successful of these congregations was that of the Oratorians, who had been at work in France since 1611. Their teaching of the Classics was not so traditional as that of the Jesuits. More stress was laid on the reading of authors than on the writing of Latin prose and verse. They taught history, including that of France. Stress was laid on mathematics and many of the Oratorian fathers were followers of Descartes— and that at a time when his philosophy was proscribed in the colleges of the University which clung to their medieval scholastic tradition. It should be added that the Oratorians were far less ultramontane in outlook than were the Jesuits. In 1790 there were all told thirty-six Oratorian colleges distributed in various parts of the country; there were also seven ex-Jesuit colleges which had been handed over to the Oratory after 1762.

It has been indicated that the colleges of the Faculty of Arts in the French universities gave what would nowadays be regarded as a secondary education and normally provided a six or eight year course ending at about the age of eighteen. After that the student could enter upon a university course proper in the Faculty of Theology, Law or Medicine. In 1789 there were twenty-one universities in France, of which eighteen possessed Arts faculties. In the University of Paris itself where, owing to the 1764 re-organisation, the number of colleges had been reduced to ten, there were about five thousand students in the Faculty of Arts; and since

1719 tuition in the University had been free. The chief criticism which had been levelled at the instruction available here was that, in spite of the influence of Descartes and the reforms initiated by Rollin in the early part of the eighteenth century, the curriculum remained traditional and antiquated. Philosophy and logic, studied in the last two years of the course, were taught parrot-fashion, and history, geography, mathematics and science, notwithstanding the general interest in these subjects among educated Frenchmen—and French women—were neglected. No wonder it was complained that youths left the Faculty of Arts 'fort ignorants'. When in 1789 the members of the 'philosophy' classes of the University of Paris sent a petition to the authorities asking that instruction might be given in French instead of Latin the request was turned down.

One stumbling-block to reform was the difficulty of finding good teachers; and although the suppression of the Society of Jesus had removed the University's chief rivals it was not able to provide a teaching personnel to equal that of the Jesuits. It was in an endeavour to rectify this state of things and to improve the qualification of teachers that in 1766 a competitive examination called the *agrégation* was instituted, and this has survived to the present day. The reform was carried out in spite of opposition from various sections of the University.

It remains to say something about university education proper at the end of the *Ancien Régime*. In 1789 the twenty-one French universities possessed eighteen faculties of theology, twenty of law, and eighteen of medicine. Here again the general criticism was that they were hampered by tradition, inimical to progress and research, and out of touch with current developments.

Expenses also tended to be heavy—especially perhaps in the faculty of medicine, where the teaching was largely theoretical. Diderot said that if a doctor were skilful at his work 'c'est à force d'assassinats'. The most popular faculty was that of law, no doubt because it provided an avenue to official posts. Many of the statesmen who became famous during the Revolution itself had received a legal training;[1] and in the year 1788–9 at Paris University as many as 563 degrees in law had been conferred.

The chief rival to the University of Paris in the field of higher education was the Collège Royal or Collège de France. It had been founded in 1530 not by any ecclesiastical authority but by the King of France, François I. Being independent of the University, it had from the beginning been less hampered by scholastic tradition, and with it had been associated such progressive scholars as Ramus and Rollin. Over the years the number of chairs from time to time had been increased and by the year 1788 there were nineteen of them. They were concerned not merely with languages—Hebrew, Greek, Latin, oriental tongues—and with French literature, but also with various departments of mathematics and sciences such as physics, chemistry, natural history, and with different branches of medicine and of law.

Professional education of a practical type was also given in seventy-two specialised institutions. They were concerned with such subjects as the military art, engineering, hydrography, mining, obstetrics, veterinary science, music and art. There were also colleges for the deaf and dumb. Other agencies of higher

[1] Of the 621 representatives of the *Tiers État* in the States-General (see below, chap. 4) no less than 360 were described as lawyers. Carlyle (*French Revolution*, chap. iv) gives their number as 374.

education outside the universities were provided by *académies*. These were learned societies of various kinds and they gave opportunity for study and research. They held discussions, published articles and 'proceedings', and encouraged branches of learning which were neglected by the universities. At the end of the *Ancien Régime* they numbered about fifty all told, and they were situated not only in Paris itself but also in many provincial towns. Most of them had been founded in the later years of the seventeenth century or the first half of the eighteenth.[1]

Such then in outline was the state of national education on the eve of the Revolution. It may be asked: what in actual fact did it all amount to? It is obvious that not inconsiderable provision *was* made for instruction at all levels from the primary school to the university or other institution of higher education; but there was equally obvious need of reform in almost every sphere. As has been said, most educational establishments were more or less directly under the control of the Church. The State had interested itself only to a very limited extent in educational matters. It certainly had provided and maintained the *écoles spéciales* which trained officers for the army or the navy or members of certain professions. It paid the professors of the Collège de France and the expenses of the Observatory and the Jardin des Plantes at Paris. This latter institution was concerned mainly with the cultivation of pharmaceutical plants and the study of their medicinal uses. But there was no kind of grant for education generally. The colleges depended on their

[1] There was an even earlier tradition of academies in France. These are dealt with in Frances Yates' treatise on *French Academies*, published by the Warburg Institute (London, 1947).

fees and endowments, and were associated with their universities or the teaching orders which ran them. All this meant that, as in the case of the various kinds of elementary school, facilities for secondary and higher education were very unevenly distributed over the country, and there was nothing in the way of a co-ordinated system of national education.

2   *Eighteenth-century criticisms of education under the Ancien Régime*

As one might expect, the educational facilities provided under the *Ancien Régime* did not escape criticism. From time to time reforms and projects had been put forward, but speaking generally they had produced no great effect. In the sixteenth and seventeenth centuries they had been concerned mainly with the universities—i.e. with secondary and higher education. The re-organisation of the University of Paris by the statutes of Henri IV[1] had revived this moribund institution after the end of the Wars of Religion, but its curriculum, its clerical character and its general spirit were but little affected. Ramus had championed the use of critical and inductive methods in philosophy, the simplifying of the classical curriculum, and the study of mathematics even to the higher and applied branches of this science. But his influence was limited by his Protestant tendencies which made him an unpopular figure in the University and ultimately led to his death in the Bartholomew massacre of 1572. The teachings of Descartes, whose *Discours de la Méthode* was published in 1637, were for the most part strongly resisted in the University of Paris, though there were not wanting individual members of it who welcomed the work and attempted to introduce it into the philosophy course. But the force of tradition was still strong, and even Charles Rollin, who was rector of the University from 1694 to 1699, was not able to effect a complete reform of it, although he did manage to introduce important

[1] See above, p. 1.

improvements in discipline; and in his *Traité des études*[1] he advocated the study of French alongside that of the Classics. Throughout the eighteenth century and right down to the outbreak of the Revolution the University of Paris remained to a large extent hampered by past traditions, and it was continually plagued by internecine quarrels concerned mainly with Jansenism, or by intervention on the part of the Parlement de Paris.

The critics to whom reference has been made above were not concerned with establishing a system of national popular education. It has already been pointed out that this had been left to voluntary effort of various kinds under the aegis of the Church. But the movement known as the 'Enlightenment', which gathered momentum as the eighteenth century progressed, had important repercussions in this field. The *philosophes*, who were responsible for this development, were advocates of the use of reason, the freedom of the individual, and the securing of his 'natural rights'. They also tended to take a utilitarian view of social institutions and to judge them by their practical value. Many of the *philosophes* regarded popular education as a key to the reforms in society which they advocated. Logically it could no longer be the prerogative of a privileged class, but it implied extension freely to all and sundry. This also meant that traditional methods and curricula would be called in question and an attempt would be made to adjust the techniques of teaching to the nature and needs of the child.

These eighteenth-century thinkers and writers who criticised the existing educational provisions in France and who proposed reforms can perhaps be divided roughly into two groups. There were those who looked

[1] 4 vols, Paris, 1726–8.

at the problem from a purely theoretical standpoint—the attitude of the philosopher, the sociologist or the politician; and there were others who proposed practical schemes for a co-ordinated national system of education, affording facilities of progress from elementary schools to institutions of higher education. Of course, any educational scheme must be based on some theoretical premises, and the second group, no less than the first, shared the philosophical views of the Enlightenment; but they went a step further and tried to apply them in definite proposals for a reformed educational system which would replace the institutions of the *Ancien Régime*.

The most famous and the most influential representative of the first group was Jean-Jacques Rousseau, whose views are set forth mainly in his *Émile*, which was published in 1762. Rousseau is not concerned with schools or class-room techniques, although a subsequent work of his, the *Considérations sur le Gouvernement de Pologne* (1782) contains a rather vague and fantastic sketch of a national and patriotic scheme of public education. But it is in *Émile*, which is couched in the form of a novel, that Rousseau's most characteristic and seminal educational theories are set forth. Looking round on the schools and colleges and universities of his day Rousseau says 'Take the very reverse of the current custom and you will nearly always do right'. He has no use for 'those ridiculous establishments called *collèges*'. Hitherto the child has been regarded as a kind of miniature adult rather than as an independent personality with his own special characteristics which determine his development and indicate his treatment. For this reason he has been subjected to a 'bookish' type of education—what Montaigne had called 'l'éducation livresque'. Rousseau says roundly 'I hate books. They only teach one to talk about things that one does not know'. He would have the child's education based on sense impressions—not on words, but as far as possible on actual experience. Rousseau was indeed—like many French thinkers of his time—influenced by the sensationalist philosophy of Locke. The child must be allowed to develop naturally according to the laws of his own being. To use Rousseau's own striking expression, we must 'allow childhood to ripen within the child'. In order to achieve this he removes the pupil from the corrupting influences of an artificialised society. Émile is brought up in the country, away from his parents and under the care and direction of a tutor who of course is Rousseau himself. There he undergoes a 'progressive' education in which each stage purports to be accommodated to the child's natural development.

It is easy to pick holes in *Émile* and to point out its paradoxes and inconsistencies. Obviously a system of educating individual children by tutors in isolation could be applied in practice to only a very limited extent, and it could never form the basis of a national system. One may also be tempted to comment that Rousseau's tutorship of the two sons of M. de Mably was, on his own showing, anything but a success. But there is no book in the whole history of education which has had a greater influence on educational theory, and therefore on educational practice. Its arresting statements, its fundamental criticisms of current methods, and the fact that they were set out in the form of a novel—all this aroused deep public interest. People were constrained to think and to undergo a radical change of mind as regards the meaning of education. *Émile* had an immediate success and has exerted an untold influence ever since not only in France, but also in every country to which western civilisation has extended. It stimulated the writing of many other treatises on education, some advocating and some opposing Rousseau's views. M. Compayré points out that during the twenty-five years which followed the publication of *Émile* there appeared in the French language twice as many books on education as during the first sixty years of the century.[1] Even in our own time new editions of this book and of Rousseau's minor educational writings, as well as treatises dealing with his views and influence, periodically appear. In short, we may regard him as the protagonist and prophet of the whole movement which bases education on child study and child psychology.

Another of those who approached the question of education from a purely theoretical point of view was the philosopher Claude-Adrien Helvétius. In his treatise *De l'esprit*, published in 1758, he out-Lockes Locke himself in asserting that all mental faculties are reducible to physical sensation. According to him all intellects are fundamentally equal and apparent inequalities are due to unequal desire for instruction. Helvétius is a utilitarian. Self-interest—love of pleasure and fear of pain—is the spring of all judgement, action and affection; social custom explains our ideas of justice and moral worth; morality, in short, is public welfare. As a reflex of his sensationalist philosophy Helvétius lays enormous stress on the influence of education as a means to this utilitarian end; and in his posthumous work *De l'homme, de ses facultés intellec-*

[1] In his *History of Pedagogy*, trans. Payne (Boston, 1886), p. 309.

tuelles et de son éducation (1772) he enounces his famous dictum 'L'Éducation peut tout'. In this term he would of course include all those influences which Sir John Adams has designated 'by-education'. Since, therefore, the character of the State will depend on the kind of education which its citizens receive, Helvétius would have a secular system of public instruction established by the civil authority. He opposed any control of education by ecclesiastics, and it was this, as much as his philosophical views, which led to a storm of protest when *De l'esprit* appeared. The book was formally condemned by the Archbishop of Paris, the Parlement de Paris and the Pope. Together with a poem by Voltaire entitled *Sur la loi naturelle*, it was torn and publicly burnt by the hangman. It was even criticised by some of those who fundamentally were on Helvétius' own side. But his sensationalist philosophy and his belief in the unique importance of educational influences had long-reaching results—particularly, perhaps, in England. His views were largely adopted by James Mill who wrote the article on 'Education' in the 1814 edition of the *Encyclopaedia Britannica*, and by Jeremy Bentham who said of Helvétius that 'he set me on the principle of utility'. The all-important influences of education and environment were also the main thesis of Robert Owen and the inspiration of his work at New Lanark.

Étienne Bonnot de Condillac was yet another *philosophe* of the period who, like Rousseau and especially Helvétius, was influenced by the philosophy of Locke. In his *Traité des sensations* (1754), however, he goes beyond his English predecessor in tracing our ideas not to the double source of sensation and reflection, but to purely empirical sensationalism alone.

Reflection is nothing but sensation 'differently transformed'. 'All our knowledge and all our faculties are
derived from the senses.'[1] Condillac wrote a number of
other philosophical works; but he had also as a young
man acted as tutor to Ferdinand, Prince of Parma, who
was a grandson of Louis XV. In connection with this
duty he worked out a *Cours d'études* (1767–75), a tedious
compilation in no less than thirteen volumes. In it he
applies his philosophical theories to education. So far
as actual practice is concerned it does not take us very
far; and in spite of his experience as a tutor Condillac
seems out of touch with the realities of child psychology.
He claims that 'the faculty of reasoning appears as our
senses begin to develop'; and in his 'leçons prélimi-
naires' therefore he expects a child of seven to be
introduced to philosophical speculations about the
nature of ideas and the operations of the mind. It is on
this foundation that the ordinary course of study is
based. Condillac certainly gives a place to Latin and
French authors, but throughout he urges the training of
the reason and decries memory work which was the
usual technique at almost every level in the educational
institutions of his day. An interesting development of
Condillac's educational views—though it does not
seem to follow directly from his philosophy—was his
advocacy of what is called the 'culture epoch theory'.
This assumes that there is a general parallelism between
the development of the human race and of the individual. For this reason the education of the child at every
stage should be related to the development of human
civilisation. 'The method I have followed', says
Condillac, 'does not resemble the usual manner of
teaching, but it is the very way in which men were led

[1] Condillac, *Œuvres* (23 vols, Paris, 1798), III, 1.

to create the arts and the sciences.'[1] This scheme was worked out later by Herbart and his followers—Ziller in particular; but as M. Compayré comments, 'It would be absurd to compel the child painfully to recommence the toil of the race'.[2] While, therefore, Condillac made a significant contribution to the Enlightenment and sketched a course of education which was a fundamental criticism of contemporary practice, it is as a philosopher, rather than as an educationist, that his influence has been chiefly exerted.

With Denis Diderot we leave the realms of pure fancy and sheer philosophical speculation and are given some practical suggestions for a scheme of education. Diderot had been educated by the Jesuits and at the Collège d'Harcourt of the University of Paris. He is of course known chiefly as the editor of the *Encyclopédie*, which is not simply a compendium of information, as its name might suggest, but a powerful criticism of existing society and an agency for its reform. It upholds the sensationalist philosophy, but it stands also for freedom of speculation and for religious toleration. The *Encyclopédie* was published between the years 1751 and 1772, and as it progressed its attacks on the despotic government of the *Ancien Régime* and on the Church, which controlled its educational institutions, became more and more marked. Attempts were made to stop the publication of this work, but its contributors included some of the most outstanding *philosophes* of the period, among them Voltaire, D'Alembert, Montesquieu, Holbach and Turgot. The article on 'Education' was written by César Chesneau Dumarsais, a gram-

---

[1] Cf. 'The genesis of knowledge in the individual must follow the same course as the genesis of knowledge in the race.' Herbert Spencer, *Education* (London, 1860), chap. II, sect. iv.

[2] *History of Pedagogy*, p. 313.

marian and a Latin scholar who had also championed the liberties of the Gallican Church. He had had some experience as a private tutor, but his contribution is a disappointing piece of work. However, the influence of the *Encyclopédie* upon education is not so much through its individual articles which touch on this subject, but through its whole spirit. It was in fact the Bible of the Age of Reason in France.

Diderot was not only its editor but he also wrote many of the contributions, especially those dealing with philosophy, the arts and industrial processes. But his reputation as an educationist, in the narrower sense, rests mainly upon a treatise entitled 'Plan of a University'. The *Encyclopédie* had brought Diderot fame rather than wealth; but the Empress Catherine II of Russia—the 'Semiramis of the North'—hearing that he was in financial difficulties, purchased his library and appointed him curator of it for the rest of his life. In 1773 she invited him to visit her, but after five months in Russia he returned to Paris. Soon after this he prepared his 'Plan of a University' which he submitted to his patroness. It is ostensibly designed for the consideration of the Russian government, but it was indirectly a criticism of existing conditions in French education. There seems to have been not much reaction to it on the part of the Russian authorities, and Diderot's treatise was not published in France until 1813–14, and then only in part. But Diderot's views have an interest in that they indicate the way in which the political and social reformers of the period were regarding educational institutions; and for that reason they are worthy of consideration.

As the title of the 'Plan' suggests, Diderot is concerned mainly with the university—the secondary education of the Faculty of Arts and the further education of the higher faculties. He does not sketch an entire co-ordinated system of popular education from the elementary stages upwards. He does, however, say that everyone from the prime minister down to the humblest peasant should know how to read, write and cipher; and he assumes the provision of free and obligatory instruction in these subjects, with even 'maintenance allowances' for those who need them. Thus he takes it for granted that entrants to the Faculty of Arts will already know how to read, write and spell, and 'how to form the digits and symbols of arithmetic—he must have learned these things at home or in the primary school.' The university will be 'open without distinction to all the children of the nation'. Its teachers are to be paid by the State and no fees are to be received from the students. Diderot lays down detailed recommendations as to the administration and discipline of colleges, the daily time-table, the qualifications of teachers and students. He even discusses such topics as text-books and school buildings. All these matters are to be a State concern, for to supervise the whole institution there is to be a general inspector of conduct and studies who is to be a 'distinguished and experienced and wise statesman'. The regulations governing the administration of the university are in the last resort to be decided by the sovereign or by her council.

In his programme for the Faculty of Arts Diderot gives pride of place to the sciences because they are of paramount value to everyone alike. He therefore classifies subjects in order of diminishing importance because he realises that not all students will complete the eight-year course—'the utility of the instruction will diminish in the same proportion as the number of my hearers diminishes'. In the first year of the Arts faculty, which pupils will enter at about the age of twelve, mathematics is the chief study. They then proceed in succeeding years by way of mechanics, hydraulics and astronomy to natural history and experimental physics. By the fifth year they are dealing with chemistry and anatomy, and in the sixth year with logic and analytical grammar. This is followed by a study of the native language; and it is not until the eighth and final year that Greek and Latin, rhetoric and poetry, are admitted. A scheme somewhat similar to this was adumbrated nearly a hundred years later by Herbert Spencer. Parallel with the complete course the pupil in the first two years is to study the first principles of metaphysics, of universal morality and of religion, which is 'only the sanction of God's will revealed and applied to natural ethics'. This is followed by a course in history (taught backwards), mythology and geography, together with the elements of economics and household management. The first-year pupils are also to have some instruction in drawing and the first principles of architecture. It seems a very ambitious and overloaded curriculum.

Of the higher faculties in contemporary universities Diderot has hardly a good word to say. Law is confined to Roman law. Civil and criminal codes, contracts, current statutes affecting property and social relations, international law—all these are completely neglected. So Diderot prescribes a four-year course in which all these subjects will be included. As for the Faculty of Theology, it is intolerant and insincere. It is chiefly concerned with unedifying quarrels—Diderot obviously had the Jansenist controversy in mind—or with perse-

26

cuting heretics. The members of the Sorbonne (as the Paris Faculty of Theology was called) are 'interfering either by disposition or through ambition. They are the least useful, the most intractable, and the most dangerous members of the State'. But Diderot does not go all the way—as did many of the *philosophes* of his day—and subscribe to Voltaire's slogan 'écrasez l'infâme'. He says with a considerable lack of enthusiasm 'The Faculty of Theology cannot be totally suppressed'; but he adds that there must be either good priests or no priests. If we must have them the State will demand that they are 'edifying, enlightened and peaceable'. It is obvious that they are to be under State control and relegated to a subordinate position.

When he comes to the Faculty of Medicine Diderot's chief criticism is that the teaching is too theoretical. The science of healing cannot be learned simply from books and lectures, and every medical school should have associated with it a hospital in which students can obtain practical experience. As it is, a young physician gains this, after qualifying, at the expense of his patients. Each medical faculty should be served by seven professors who between them will cover all the branches of the subject, and the course itself will last seven years.

Diderot, like most of the *philosophes*, is not primarily an educationist, and his works dealing with a system of public instruction are not the most important of his writings. But he was extraordinarily versatile and whatever he says is at any rate of interest. He is an enlightened critic of some of his contemporaries; he sees the weakness of Rousseau's 'negative' education and realises the importance of positive instruction; he is a convinced exponent of the paramount importance of science in the secondary school course, but this does not make him a bigoted opponent of literary studies. He was himself an enthusiastic admirer of Homer. In his *Réfutation suivie de l'ouvrage d'Helvétius intitulé l'Homme*[1] he combats the author's exaggerations as to the all-powerful influence of education. He drives home his arguments with an illustration suggested perhaps by the Parable of the Sower. He says that for thousands of years the rain has fallen upon the rocks without making them fertile; and if seed is sown there it will never germinate and grow, even though suitable moisture is provided. As to religious teaching, Diderot does not exclude it from the university, but the State is to have the final control in Church matters. For this reason he would oppose the unification of the Orthodox Church in Russia with the Roman Catholic communion. That would imply a 'foreign head' for the Russian Church. 'There should be no appeal', he says, 'other than to the Sovereign, no council outside the Empire, no head of the council other than the head of the State'; and this obviously would imply a condemnation of ultra-montane tendencies in the Church of France.

[1] *Œuvres* (20 vols, 1875–7), II, 275 ff.

3   Pre-Revolution projects for a national system of education

We come now to consider those reformers who were less interested in the theoretical and philosophical aspects of education, but who wished to get rid of the existing unco-ordinated provision, controlled more or less directly at every level by the Church, and to replace it by a system organised and supervised by the State. They are in the main men of affairs, statesmen, parliamentarians and politicians. We shall meet this type again when considering the educational proposals which were put forward during the period of the Revolution itself.

One of the most distinguished of these in the middle period of the eighteenth century was the lawyer Louis-René Caradeuc de la Chalotais, who for many years was a dominating influence in the Parlement de Rennes. In the course of events which led up to the expulsion of the Jesuits from France the various *parlements* were required to examine the constitutions of the religious orders which were established in the area where they had jurisdiction. It was thus that the constitutions of the Society of Jesus came under review, and the resulting reports were known as *comptes rendus*. In December 1761 La Chalotais laid before the Parlement de Rennes, which was concerned with the province of Brittany, his *Compte rendu des constitutions des Jésuites*. Other provincial *parlements* submitted similar reports to much the same effect, though that of La Chalotais was probably the most outstanding of them and it contributed powerfully to the suppression of the Order in France in 1762. In his *Compte rendu* he inveighs against a society which is not only a close and independent corporation but also has an ultramontane outlook. The religious orders in general have been largely responsible for the theological and political quarrels which for long have been distracting the country. La Chalotais would not necessarily debar ecclesiastics entirely from educational work—he has a good word to say for the Oratorians—but he claims for the nation a system of education which depends on the State alone and belongs to the State and not to the Church. 'Every nation', he says, 'has an inalienable and imprescriptible right to instruct its members, and the children of the State should be educated by members of the State.' Education should therefore be in the hands of teachers and administrators who are primarily Frenchmen both by birth and choice, and whose first loyalty will be to the State and not to some religious order or ultramontane authority.

At the same time La Chalotais seems less concerned with the training and qualification of teachers than one might have expected. He gives a somewhat exaggerated importance to the use of suitable text-books. 'I ask', he says, 'for books that would be easy to write and would perhaps dispense with the necessity for having teachers'; and he calls upon the King to have such text-books prepared. They would 'constitute the best instruction that teachers could give and they would replace every other teaching method...If these books were well composed there would be no need of trained teachers, and there would no longer be any reason for disputing about their qualifications.' It is easy to criticise these recommendations and to comment that a State education imparted from inspired text-books is hardly likely to be technically an improvement on a Church-sponsored education imparted by members of a religious order, trained and dedicated to the work of teaching.

It remains true that there was a lack of books suitable for use in schools, and any real advance in education implied supplying this need. As has been pointed out, in the *petites écoles* it had been customary to teach the elements of reading from Latin words in religious manuals or from catechisms. There was little available reading matter such as would appeal to children, and the average elementary school, of whatever type, would hardly be able to afford to supply its pupils with individual copies of such works as the Fables of La Fontaine or the Quartrains of Pibrac. In the *collèges* classical texts, such as those *in usum Delphini*[1] were the staple of instruction. Treatises on history, geography, mathematics, the sciences—subjects which the revolutionary educationists wished to stress—although not lacking were hard to come by. Again it must be remembered that La Chalotais was legislating for an abnormal situation. The expulsion of the Society of Jesus from France meant that there was an enormous shortage of efficient teachers and that some urgent steps would be needed to fill the gaps. Some of the vacant colleges of the Jesuits were taken over by the

---

[1] The 'Delphine Classics' were editions of Latin authors prepared during the seventeenth century ostensibly for the use of the Grand Dauphin, son of Louis XIV and pupil of Bossuet (see H. C. Barnard, *The French Tradition in Education*, London, 1922, pp. 136–7). They were much used by classical scholars all over Europe. On the whole subject of school text-books during the Revolution period see the Fortescue Tracts (London, 1899), 368; C. Hippeau, *L'Instruction publique en France pendant la Révolution*, II, 48–9, and the article in F. Buisson, *Dictionnaire de pédagogie* (2 vols, Paris, 1888), II, 1604–8.

Oratorians who were a definitely 'French' order without ultramontane affiliations, and that is why La Chalotais exempts them from any general condemnation of the teaching orders.

In 1763 La Chalotais became involved in a quarrel between the Parlement de Rennes and the Duc d'Aiguillon who was the royal governor of the province of Brittany. As a result of this he was imprisoned in the citadel of St Malo, though he was later released and exiled to Saintes, in Saintonge, where he remained for ten years. But when Louis XVI came to the throne in 1774 La Chalotais was recalled and granted an indemnity. Before his incarceration he had already, in 1763, published his *Essai d'éducation nationale ou plan d'études pour la jeunesse*. It amplifies and applies the principles which had been laid down in the *Compte rendu*. In the *Essai* La Chalotais turns from destructive criticism to a detailed scheme for a national system which is to replace the institution which he condemned and which is now being abolished. Perhaps his actual recommendations are less significant than his general policy. For pupils from the age of about five or six to ten he wants a curriculum which will 'appeal to the senses', and he includes in this category history, geography, natural history and 'physical and mathematical recreations'. He assumes that the child has already learnt to read, write and draw, though he thinks that research is needed on methods of teaching reading. The Fables of La Fontaine are to be learned by heart. Alongside of this work dancing and music (for 'all persons above the common people'), walks, excursions and leisure-time occupations are prescribed. One is perhaps a little surprised to find that La Chalotais seems here to hedge on the subject of popular education, though his

32

views were shared by many of his contemporaries, including Rousseau and Voltaire. He thinks that we should beware of over-educating the children of working-class parents, lest there should be a shortage of recruits for the manual trades and for agricultural labour. For this reason La Chalotais condemns the Christian Brothers who 'teach reading and writing to people who ought to learn nothing beyond how to use a plane or a file, but are no longer willing to do so... The welfare of society requires that the education of the common people should not go beyond its occupations.'[1]

In a somewhat similar vein La Chalotais thinks that it is better to have fewer colleges, provided that they are good, and fewer students, provided that they are better taught. About the age of ten, therefore, after the preliminary course more serious studies begin. The Classics are given an important place, but with them goes an equal attention to French authors. 'It is shameful', says La Chalotais, 'that in a system of education for France French literature should be neglected, as though we did not have enough models in our own language.' Such studies are at once food for the mind and also the 'enlightenment and adornment of the world'. La Chalotais' criticism is that contemporary *collèges* have treated them in a narrow and formal way, but they should conduce to the inculcation of good taste. History, geography, and mathematics are continued at the secondary stage, and with them goes 'the

[1] The *intendants* also tended to discourage popular education. The following comment by one of them is not untypical: 'A peasant who knows how to read and write leaves agriculture in order to learn a craft or become a tradesman. This is a very great evil.' (Refer to F. Ponteil, *Histoire de l'enseignement en France*, Paris, 1966, pp. 37–8.)

study of nature from nature itself', together with some contact with industrial arts and manufactures. Finally, as a training in accurate thinking and reasoning there will come a course in logic, metaphysics and moral philosophy. Thus La Chalotais outlines a co-ordinated course from the age of about five or six to seventeen or eighteen; but perhaps because he is drawing up a scheme to replace the Jesuit *collèges* he is particularly concerned with secondary education. He does not deal with the higher faculties of the university.

Although La Chalotais condemns an ecclesiastical system of education he is no opponent of religion. He believes that it is the duty of State schools to give instruction in fundamental ethical truths, but he would leave definite religious teaching to the churches and the family. 'Is it possible', he says, 'to make a purely philosophic religion or a national religion? Would not a religion without worship destroy itself?' The duties of the parish priest should include not only the teaching of religious observances, but also simple instruction in how to avoid and cure common ailments, and explanations of the laws so far as the members of his flock are affected by them. All classes in the State should realise that esteem is gained by being useful and helpful, and that true religion consists in imitating Him who went about doing good—*pertransibat beneficiendo*.

La Chalotais is the antithesis of that paradoxical genius Rousseau, and he can hardly be classed as a *philosophe* like Helvétius, Condillac, or even Diderot. He is a practical man of affairs and a 'bonny fighter', whether he is championing the Parlement de Rennes against the governor D'Aiguillon, or whether he is belabouring the Society of Jesus. As has been said, his *Compte rendu* was an important factor in the downfall of the Jesuits, and to a contemporary observer it might have seemed to be La Chalotais' chief title to fame. Indeed, its importance was immediately recognised and within a year or two it had been translated into Dutch, German and Russian. But in the long run it is the *Essai d'éducation nationale* which has proved of the greater significance. It powerfully reinforced the growing conviction, not only among parliamentarians but also among progressive thinkers everywhere, that education is a State concern. This conviction is the inspiration of almost every plan of education which was put forward henceforth, not only in the period immediately preceding the Revolution, but still more during the Revolution itself. It was the principle upon which the Napoleonic 'University' was founded, and it has been adopted, more or less completely, not only in France but in every other civilised country. It thus happened that within a year of the publication of Rousseau's *Émile* there appeared another educational document of hardly less importance. Between them they revolutionised the philosophy and techniques of education and also its administration.

Passing reference should perhaps be made to the work of two other educational reformers who, like La Chalotais, were administrators and not primarily philosophers or educationists. The first of them, Rolland d'Erceville, had taken an active part in the attack on the Society of Jesus. He had even published at his own expense a treatise entitled *Assertions dangereuses et pernicieuses soutenues par les Jésuites*, which indicates his attitude towards them. As president of the Parlement de Paris he presented to it in 1768 a report which outlines a scheme for an organised system of education to meet the new situation. He wants to ensure that every class in society will receive the type of instruction appropriate to it. 'Every type of soil does not need the same treatment, nor does it produce the selfsame crop; every mind does not require the same degree of culture; all men have not the same needs or abilities, and it is in proportion to these needs and abilities that public education should be regulated.' Everyone should of course learn to read and write, for these subjects are the key to all other instruction. Like La Chalotais, Rolland distrusts ecclesiastics as teachers; they are more likely to consult the interests of their order than their duties as citizens of the State. With a view, therefore, to securing the right kind of teachers he proposes the formation of a normal school in which they will be adequately trained. It will be staffed by professors drawn from the various university faculties, and instruction will be given not only in academic subjects, but also in the actual art of teaching. The national system of public instruction is to be put under the control of a central authority situated in Paris—a department of the government to which Rolland gives the title Bureau de Correspondance.

The national system which is to give effect to Rolland's theories is to be organised in four stages of instruction: village schools teaching the three 'R's'; *demi-collèges* dealing with the elements of religion and ethics, together with some instruction in Latin, French and history; *collèges de plein exercice*[1] giving the full course of the Faculty of Arts; and universities with the higher faculties. Private educational establishments are not forbidden, but they are to be rigorously super-

---

[1] Under the *Ancien Régime* 'collège de plein exercice' had been used as a technical term for a college which provided all the ordinary classes of the Arts faculty and also the two classes of philosophy. Refer to note on p. 8.

vised. 'All masters of boarding-schools and others who keep schools shall not be allowed to teach publicly unless they have obtained permission from the college of the area in which they are situated; and this permission shall be given only after an examination to which the principal and the teachers will be submitted.' Taken as a whole, then, Rolland's scheme—so he claims—will engender a sense of national solidarity and break down provincial barriers. It will be 'the only means of reviving love of the fatherland'.

The other scheme to which reference has been made was suggested by the statesman and economist Anne-Robert-Jacques Turgot. He had been educated at the University of Paris and was intended for an ecclesiastical career, but he decided instead to become a lawyer. In 1761 he was appointed *intendant* of the district of Limoges where he introduced reforms in the assessment and collection of taxes, and developed public works. Thirteen years later he obtained the important position of Controleur Général des Finances. His appointment won the enthusiastic approval of Condorcet. 'Never', he said, 'has there entered any royal council a man who unites to so high a degree virtue, courage, disinterestedness, concern for public welfare, and the zeal to secure it.'

Turgot was one of the chief exponents of a school of philosophers and economists known as physiocrats. They advocated the freedom of the individual so far as it was consistent with the rights of others, and they regarded government as necessary, but believed that its influence should be restricted within the narrowest possible limits. They held that commerce is an unproductive activity and laid stress on the importance of agriculture; the individual should be entitled to the fruits of his own labour, and therefore property was a sacred right. They believed in education for all. Turgot himself said 'I am convinced that men cannot become more happy except by becoming more reasonable; but unfortunately the greater part of them are plunged in the depths of ignorance and in a stupidity which renders them unhappy and dangerous, because they can on the one hand so easily be oppressed and on the other deceived'.[1]

Although Turgot's liberal views and projects of reform won the admiration of many of the *philosophes*, they roused animosity in other quarters. Finally, in 1776, Louis XVI was induced to dismiss him. However, in the previous year he had presented to the King a memorial on the organisation of municipalities, and this contained some observations on a scheme of education. As far as general principles are concerned Turgot's views have much in common with those of Rolland. He is very conscious of the paramount importance of education in the life of the State, because it provides the means of instructing future citizens in their duties and responsibilities. To impart such moral and social instruction he believes, like La Chalotais, that special text-books will be needed, and these should be composed with the greatest care. Also in every parish there should be a schoolmaster who will use these books in his teaching and who will also give instruction in reading, writing, arithmetic, mensuration and the elements of mechanics. Turgot does not indicate any details of a State-organised system of education, but he would leave these to be determined by a royal Council of National Education, under the direction of which would be placed all the academies, universities,

[1] *Œuvres* (9 vols, Paris, 1808), VII, 396.

colleges and primary schools in the kingdom. Circumstances rendered it difficult for the King to take any
action on Turgot's recommendations; and when the
royal support was withdrawn he had to retire from
public affairs. But the adhesion of so eminent a statesman and thinker was yet another influence to strengthen
the general feeling on the part of *philosophes* and parliamentarians alike that the only solution was the assumption by the State of responsibility for education at all
levels; and this contributed to proposals which were
put forward during the period of the Revolution itself.

A more complete scheme for a system of school
education was suggested almost on the eve of the
Revolution by one who was neither a *philosophe* nor a
parliamentarian. Louis Philipon de la Madelaine had
certainly been trained as a lawyer and he held one or
two official positions; but it was as a rather dilettante
litterateur that he won some contemporary notice.
Although he had to go into hiding at the outbreak of the
Revolution he was eventually given the post of librarian
to the Ministry of the Interior under the Convention,
and he survived to the age of eighty with a pension
granted at the Restoration. His published works include
plays and songs, treatises on legal and social subjects,
guide books, grammars and dictionaries. But it is in his
Vues patriotiques sur l'éducation du peuple (1783) and
De l'éducation des collèges (1784) that his educational
proposals are set forward. For some reason or other
Philipon seems to have been generally overlooked by
historians of French education, even in his own country;
and therefore no apology, perhaps, is needed for
dealing with his scheme in rather greater detail than
with some of those to which reference has already been
made.

The national system which he envisages has something in common with that which existed in England during the latter part of the nineteenth century. There are two quite distinct streams—one of elementary, and the other of secondary, education. The former is designed for those whom Philipon calls *le peuple*—the class which has to earn its living by 'travaux mercenaires, manuels et serviles'. The children of the leisured or professional classes or the *bourgeoisie* will be educated in *collèges*; and for them an entirely different type of course is prescribed. Philipon realises that there are exceptional individuals who from time to time may manage to rise above the working class; but if so he says definitely that they cease to be *peuple* for the purpose of his definition. In any case, no scheme is suggested whereby gifted children may be assisted to pass from the elementary stream to that provided by the *collèges*.

The wise education of the 'people' is regarded as of extreme national importance, because, although contemporary discontents and revolutionary ideas may be due to the ambition of the great, it is the force supplied by the 'people' that puts these ideas into execution. Because the lower classes have nothing to lose they are always ready to risk everything. So Philipon believes that the State will benefit if such persons receive education—but it must be education of the right sort. He complains that existing institutions of the 'elementary' type are too often run by 'grammarians', who give instruction of an entirely unsuitable literary character. This does indeed tend to lead the 'people' to despise manual labour on the farm or in the workshop, and tempt them to become lackeys or monks. So the test is to teach children of this class what will be useful to them when they grow up, and to restrict their curriculum rigidly to this. Here Philipon's attitude is rather like that of La Chalotais.

If then the proper education of the 'people' is of so great importance to the welfare of the State, it cannot be left to private initiative; it must become a public responsibility. Philipon makes it quite clear that the expense of a national system of elementary education must be borne by the government. Working-class parents will not be able to pay for their children's education: 'Si le gouvernement n'y subvient pas, qui en fera la dépense?' It is also the case too often that such parents are little interested in education and do not value it. This would imply that even if schooling were made free it would also be necessary to render it compulsory. Philipon does not make this point specifically, but it is certainly implied in what he says. He envisages a school-life of six years at most—from the age of six for as long as the pupil can profit, but not beyond twelve; but complete freedom from school is to be allowed during harvest or at other times when child labour in the country is needed. Eight months in the year is sufficient for school attendance. Philipon seems to imply that the child will be a boarder and not a day pupil.

The problem of financing such a system of public elementary education is to be met primarily by entrusting it to the teaching orders. Philipon says that he is not concerned which particular order it is, so long as it does not teach 'langues, lettres et sciences'. He doubtless has the Brothers of the Christian Schools in mind. He feels that members of such orders tend to be better trained than the average country *maître d'école*; the reputation of the order itself also provides a stimulus, and far less expense in the way of salary, etc., will be entailed, especially as such teachers are celibates. Philipon estimates that there are in existence about 41,000 'little schools', and each *maître d'école* receives an average salary of 400 livres. This represents an outlay of 16,400,000 livres which would go far to meet the cost of a national system worked by members of the teaching orders. If extra funds are needed they can be met by drawing on the confiscated revenues of the Society of Jesus, by enforcing levies on various legal processes, by the taxation of luxuries, by a duty on the baptism of children of the well-to-do or on the first-year revenue of an ecclesiastical benefice, or by special church collections. The working of the whole system will be entrusted in each diocese to a Bureau d'Administration des Écoles du Peuple. It will consist of ten 'notables', with the Bishop as president. One of their duties will be the periodic inspection of the schools for which they are responsible. As La Chalotais had said, their aim should be to provide few schools, but good ones. It will be enough to have one school for a group of thirty or forty *communautés* according to the population; but each should have a staff of four masters who will be paid an annual salary of 300 livres and receive a pension after thirty or thirty-five years of service.

Like Locke, Philipon lays great stress on physical education and hygienic school environment as an essential preliminary to any kind of intellectual training. He believes that children who are destined to become manual labourers should be hardened off early. Their food should be frugal and consist mainly of rye bread, water and fruits. Their clothing should be sufficient, but simple, and they are to go barefoot and bare-headed. As for beds, these are forbidden. The children will sleep on the floor or on the table, fully dressed and without coverings or mattresses. The school buildings will be away from towns, in a healthy position and surrounded by grounds. Many country monasteries could easily be converted into public elementary schools. It is desirable to have a river or lake in the neighbourhood because regular open-air cold baths and swimming are an essential part of the curriculum. Cleanliness is the best preventive of illness—hence the necessity for keeping the hair short, ensuring fresh air in the class-rooms and disinfecting them by fumigation with vinegar, juniper, or gunpowder. Eight hours sleep is prescribed; children go to bed at 8.0 p.m. and rise at 4.0. a.m. Athletics and gymnastic exercises are of great importance, but one should avoid those in which the children have to push each other or hold their heads downwards. An upright posture, with the chest out and the shoulders back, is to be inculcated. In short, the body is the means by which the worker gets his living, and it is of the first importance therefore to develop in the child a strong physical constitution.

As far as intellectual education goes Philipon would restrict children of the 'people' to a very limited curriculum. However, he regards a knowledge of reading as important, and pupils should learn to decipher not only printed books but also manuscripts. The use of written material in the teaching of reading was not an uncommon custom. In the contemporary 'little schools' children were sometimes encouraged to bring copies of leases, contracts, indentures, or other legal documents from home in order to assist in this process; and it doubtless had a practical value for the peasant or artisan who might conceivably become the victim of sharp practice without a knowledge of this kind. Fairy tales and fables are forbidden in the reading lesson, but simple treatises on farming, first-aid and useful arts are to be specially recommended. As for writing, Philipon considers it to be of doubtful value to the working-classes. Here he is obviously influenced by contemporary theories and practice. As has been mentioned, in elementary schools—particularly those in the country and those for girls—writing was by no means always taught; or it might be regarded as an 'extra' for which an additional fee was demanded. Philipon feels that a 'superficial notion' is sufficient; and by that he seems to mean the power to sign one's name legibly, because the use of a cross or mark may facilitate falsification. All this has a bearing on the value of Maggiolo's statistics.

The four rules of arithmetic, practical geometry and drawing are useful to the farmer or the artisan because they can be applied in the measuring of fields in constructional work. In teaching these subjects the master will use the walls of his class-room as a blackboard. Some information as to practical medicine and the recognition and use of drug-plants should be given; and in country schools also pupils should be taught the care of animals and their treatment in illness. With this should go some very simple scientific instruction, so that pupils may learn, for example, to recognise the cardinal points by the pole-star, and may not be alarmed by such natural phenomena as thunder-storms and eclipses. In order to promote habits of cheerfulness, which will counteract the rigour and monotony of a life of manual labour, children while at school should be encouraged to sing. When they enter or leave the classroom, or when they go out on an expedition, let them do so to the sound of music. 'Tambour, clarinette, fifre ou hautbois' are prescribed, though there is no indication as to who performs on these instruments or how and where the skill is acquired. However, of the four masters allocated to each elementary school one is given charge of physical education and music. Of the others, one teaches the three 'R's', one drawing and geometry, and one medicine and the veterinary art. All alike are responsible for the inculcation of morality and religion.

To this last-mentioned subject Philipon consecrates a whole section of his treatise. The chief weaknesses of the labouring classes are fear due to ignorance, temptation to steal, intemperance and idleness. At school punishments may be necessary, but corporal punishments should be forbidden. It may be necessary to exclude an offender from games or excursions; but as far as possible moral teaching should be effected by an appeal to the child's reason or sense of honour. Pupils should be encouraged to give help in times of emergency or danger. Praise the courageous and blame the cowardly. Point out that those who will not work will be reduced to beggary and may starve. Stress the degrading aspect of drunkenness and the dangers of over-indulgence to the health of the drunkard and the well-being of his family. Since members of the family depend largely on one another they should be encouraged to help one another in times of distress. The 'people' have their 'honour' as well as the upper classes; but with the latter it is being ashamed of doing evil, whereas with the former it should be the tradition of doing good. As to religion itself Philipon has little to say. It is, however, an indispensable necessity for the 'people' because it affords their chief restraint against wrong-doing and it provides a consolation for the troubles that are inherent in their estate. Religious teaching must therefore be provided in school, and the diocesan catechism is prescribed for this purpose. Children should say their prayers every day and attend Mass on Sundays and Church festivals. But there the matter ends for them. They are not to take part in pilgrimages or join confraternities; and they are to take religious dogmas on trust and not ask for explanations.

Philipon realises that education does not end when one leaves school, and he even recommends that government inspectors should have the special duty of supervising young people of the labouring classes up to the age of, say, twenty-five. Physical exercises are to be organised, country festivals with processions, music and dancing, are to be encouraged. Nor should intellectual education be neglected. In towns and villages alike some accommodation should be made available for what in England at a later date would have been called a Mechanics' Institute. Specimens of simple scientific apparatus, books on agriculture and the care of animals, would be kept here; and in this way some sort of technical education would be fostered. Philipon even recommends that the *curé* from time to time, instead of the usual sermon at Mass, should give a talk on agriculture or other matters of practical value to his parishioners. He is even to hold special classes for each sex in order to give instruction on appropriate behaviour during courtship, the problems of early married life, the hygiene of childbirth, and similar subjects which seem singularly inappropriate for a lecturer who has taken a vow of celibacy.

Like Rousseau in his *Émile*, Philipon adds a kind of appendix on the education of women. He quotes the example of Sparta and advances the usual argument that to produce strong and healthy children the

46

mothers themselves must be women of good physique. Bodily exercises are therefore as important, though not necessarily so strenuous, for girls as for boys. Unhealthy fashions, such as the use of corsets or heavy head-dresses, are to be avoided. Intellectual education is of minor importance for women, and a school-life of only three years (seven or eight to ten or eleven) is recommended. The curriculum should be limited to the three 'R's', which are useful in the business of house-keeping; and of course girls must learn needle-work and domestic duties. As a relaxation they may be allowed to sing and dance; but there must be no emphasis on *agrémens du corps*. The destiny of the girl of the labouring class is to work hard and therefore the nearer the education of the women of the 'people' approximates to that of the men, the more perfect it will be.

Such then is the national system of popular education which Philipon wishes to see organised by the government. It is confined definitely to the children of the 'lower classes', who are to be prepared specifically for their particular function in society. But in his second treatise *De l'éducation des collèges*, which appeared in 1784, he deals with schooling for the other section of society. Philipon would abolish the 'little schools' and set their *maîtres d'école* free for more useful work. Instead he would devote the first seven years of the child's life to physical development. With a reminiscence of Rousseau he advocates that nature should be allowed to strengthen children's bodies by means of fresh air and liberty of movement. There should be no restraint except to prevent harm.

The college course should be remodelled so as to admit the child at the age of seven, and to start his education with the elements which hitherto had been taught in the *petites écoles*. Much stress is laid on healthy classroom conditions, and Philipon repeats the hygienic measures which he recommended in his former treatise. Children are to do their work standing—even when they are writing; though if necessary and as a concession they may be allowed to prop themselves up, as canons do in their cathedral stalls. School hours will be from 7.30 a.m. to 11.30 a.m., and from 1.30 p.m. to 5 p.m. No lesson will last longer than an hour and between each of them there will be an interval of fifteen minutes. The only holidays are on every Thursday and on Church festivals; but in the former case an elaborate system of activities is organised. Children are to assemble at 8.0 a.m. and go off, in charge of a master, to bathe and learn swimming or to take part in gymnastic exercises. In the afternoon there will be country excursions and the responsible teacher will give instruction in botany or mineralogy or in identifying birds. The staff must not complain of being overworked—teachers are made for pupils, and not pupils for teachers.

Philipon thinks that for the average pupil an eight-year course from the age of seven to fifteen is sufficient. He deprecates the custom of some of the teaching orders (e.g. the Oratorians) whereby the same master accompanies his form throughout their school career. He prefers the arrangement which obtains in the Faculty of Arts at Paris, where every class has its own special staff. He works out a scheme of organisation by which each *collège* would have thirteen masters, including a principal and a *préfet* who between them are responsible for the administration, discipline, syllabus and arrangement of studies. After thirty years of service teachers will become 'emeritus', and will retire with a pension; but they may be called upon to replace existing staff who are off duty, or to help out in an emergency.

Philipon's most drastic innovations concern the actual curriculum of the *collège*. Grammar, he says, is a most abstract study: 'la science de l'homme fait'. It is absurd therefore to make it the basis of the education of children. It may be necessary to give language work an important part in the college curriculum, but the existing emphasis on Latin is mistaken. We are not educating pupils solely for the professions of theology, law and medicine. So our author would give a prominent place to modern languages; and here 'practice' is the operative word. Philipon is in fact an advocate of the Direct Method. Even Latin can be taught in this way, as the oft-quoted case of Montaigne reminds us.

An interesting section of *De l'éducation des collèges* deals with the time-table and general layout of the eight-year course. The child comes to school at the age of seven having had so far no formal intellecual instruction. In the first year therefore it is necessary to begin with the teaching of reading and writing. Two hours a day are devoted to each subject. As in the elementary schools, the classroom walls can be used as blackboards. Two hours a day also at this stage are to be given to drawing, which will be of far greater use to the average citizen than a knowledge of Latin. It is in the second year of the course that language work will begin; and the language to be studied is not Latin, but Italian. This, says Philipon, is 'le plus facile des idioms qui nous environnent'. Four periods a day are prescribed, but the books used should be varied—sometimes a historian, sometimes a poet, sometimes a moralist. And he makes it clear that in studying a foreign language, if it is properly taught, one is learning to express oneself, whether orally or in writing, in one's own vernacular. So a special stress is given to this work in the second form, and the only other subject on the time-table is drawing to which again two hours a day are devoted.

In the third class a second foreign language is begun; and this will either be English or German, according to the part of France in which the *collège* is situated. Here again four hours a day are given to the subject, and Italian is abandoned after only one year of study. The other two hours are devoted to geography which is necessary not only for the traveller, but also for understanding the *Gazette du Jour*. Philipon anticipates modern technique by recommending the use of the globe in order to teach earth movements, and he would include lessons on the history of geography and accounts of discovery and travels. It is not until the fourth year of the course that Latin becomes the main subject of the curriculum. As before, four hours a day are given to it, and the other two periods are earmarked for what Philipon calls 'experimental physics'. He gives no particulars as to what should be included under this subject, but is content to leave these to the specialist teacher. Latin is continued in the fifth year, but now the subsidiary subject is chemistry. For science teaching a special classroom, equipped with suitable apparatus, will be necessary. In Class VI Latin is again the basic subject, with two periods a day of mathematics. Thus a three-year course in Latin, with twenty hours a week given to it, is provided in Philipon's scheme; so that, in spite of the drastic reforms proposed and the comminution of the curriculum as regards the other subjects, the foundation of the *collège* course, so far as it has one, is still classical.

As with the contemporary colleges of the Faculty of Arts and the teaching orders, Philipon rounds off his eight-year course with two years of 'philosophy'. However, he recommends some changes in the existing procedure. For example, he points out that it is illogical that the 'rhetoric' year should precede that given to philosophy proper. *L'art de bien penser* should obviously pave the way for *l'art de bien dire*. Barren exercises, like the reduction of syllogisms, should be banished from the philosophy course; but it should include three months of logic, one of metaphysics, four of ethics, and four of general physics. As usual, four periods a day are given to this main subject, and the subsidiary this time is economics. This latter should be no theoretical study of national housekeeping, but definitely oriented towards the practical business of running a home or administering an estate. Finally, in the eighth year of the course, rhetoric becomes the special study. It will be taught in French and attention should be given to grammar, to figures of speech, and to written compositions. The understanding and appreciation of poetry are certainly important, but setting children to compose verses is a barren and mechanical business. As a foil to the rhetoric course two hours a day are to be given either to commerce or to arts and crafts. The former subject is more suited to schools which are situated in towns and where many of the pupils are destined to become business men. Instruction should be given in such subjects as foreign exchanges, book-keeping, and stocks and shares. Country schools will find it better to teach arts and crafts, though Philipon does not suggest any details of the course which he proposes. He recommends however that the pupils should follow up their work by visits on Thursday afternoons to factories, workshops, dockyards and other places where various types of constructional work are being carried on.

Such then is the course proposed. As will be seen, it comprises most of the subjects which would be taught in a modern grammar school, though for the most part they are dealt with in a scrappy and unconnected way. History does not appear as a specific subject on the time-table, but Philipon contents himself with saying that it should be associated with the study of languages. The books used in the classes of Italian, English or German, and Latin will always include historical works, so that the two subjects will be studied simultaneously. Similarly, as in the elementary school, religion is an important subject, but it does not appear on the time-table. It should permeate the whole of the day's work. All the same, half an hour a week may be devoted to specific religious instruction. In addition to the catechism, passages from Bourdaloue and Bossuet may be studied. Religious observances should not be overdone, and care should be taken to avoid stressing lugubrious topics, such as Purgatory, Hell and the Last Judgement. 'Faîtes de l'Être suprême un père et non un tyran.'

It is obvious that Philipon de la Madelaine owes something to his predecessors—particularly perhaps to Rousseau and La Chalotais; but in his practical and detailed suggestions for a national system of school education he makes a contribution all his own. Philipon has no theoretical or political axe to grind; and his scheme, in spite of some obvious weaknesses, is fundamentally a common sense one. When the city of Marseilles laid its *cahier des doléances*[1] before the States-General in 1789 it demanded a system of public

[1] See below, pp. 54–5.

education 'based on the patriotic views of M. Philipon de la Madelaine'. In January 1795 also he was included among a number of savants to each of whom the Convention granted a subsidy of 3000 livres on the grounds that their work had contributed 'à soulager l'humanité, à éclairer les hommes ou à perfectionner les arts utiles'.

4 The States-General. The cahiers. Mirabeau's educational project

By the latter part of the eighteenth century France was practically bankrupt. The various attempts at financial reform made by statesmen such as Turgot, Necker, Calonne and Brienne were powerless against the opposition of the nobility and the clergy who clung to their exemptions and privileges. But this attitude had aroused great resentment, and theories of political liberty and social equality had been emphasised by the teachings of the *philosophes* and the encyclopaedists. France's intervention in the American War of Independence had also stimulated the spread of republican ideas. The only solution seemed to be the abolition of abuses and a just distribution of taxation. The whole situation was complicated by a bread shortage, due largely to the very poor harvest of 1788. In the face of the general discontent the King, Louis XVI, remained vacillating and powerless, and his most unpopular queen, Marie Antoinette, interfered on behalf of her favourites and exercised her considerable influence to oppose reform. At last, after some abortive attempts, the King consented to convoke the States-General—a kind of national parliament in which the three 'estates', clergy, nobility and commons, were represented. It had not been summoned since 1614.

As a preliminary to this step, every electoral body of each of the states alike, which sent its representatives to this Assembly, was entitled to submit an address to the Crown, setting forth its grievances and its proposals for reform. These documents are called *cahiers de doléances*.

54

They are chiefly concerned with the abolition of fiscal inequality and seignorial dues, and they show a general desire for a moderate reform and the drawing up of a written constitution. But some of them also contain criticisms of the existing educational provision in the area which they represent; and they put forth proposals for its reform. In spite of their previous attitude, the privileged classes are beginning to see the red light. Many of the *cahiers* of the nobility, and particularly of the clergy, refer to educational matters. For example, the *noblesse* of Lyons ask for an education for both sexes alike which will foster a 'national character'. Those of Paris express the view that education should be 'perfected and extended to all classes of citizens'. At Saint-Mihiel they assert that 'national education is perhaps the most important object which can be set before the States-General'. The *noblesse* of Blois want a national council to draw up a scheme of State education and to secure the compilation of elementary text-books which will help pupils to know and respect the laws. Similarly, the clergy of Bar-sur-Seine say that there is no subject which needs the more urgent attention of the States-General than national education, and they ask it to produce a 'salutary plan for this, which is so universally desired'. The clergy of Rodez and Saumur also recommend the formation of a corps of teachers, established and organised by the State. Instances of this kind could be multiplied.

It remains true however that, though it is by no means lacking, there is less articulate demand for a national educational system on the part of the Third Estate. It has been suggested that the reason for this is that the *cahiers* of the commons were not drawn up by peasants and artisans, most of whom might be illiterate, but by some more educated person—perhaps a member of the *bourgeoisie*, who of course would also belong to the *Tiers État*. It must be remembered also that, in addition to manual workers and agriculturists, this order included the professional classes such as lawyers, civil servants, doctors, writers, and also merchants and traders and their clerks. The latter group might contain many who, like La Chalotais and Voltaire, did not believe in popular education. The *bourgeoisie* generally were more interested in achieving a status of political equality and it is probable that the peasantry were primarily concerned with the acquirement of some measure of civil liberty and with relief from the excessive taxation, *corvées*, and other burdens to which Arthur Young refers in his *Travels in France*. They might often remain content with the not wholly inadequate, if elementary, provision of education for children of their class. In some cases it would appear also that the fear of added financial responsibility, which might be incurred, made petitioners unwilling to ask for a more extended provision of popular schools.

No sooner had the States-General assembled than difficulties began to arise. They were concerned chiefly with the proportion of representatives from each order and the method of voting; but finally it was secured that there should be 308 deputies from the clergy, 285 from the nobility, and 621 for the *Tiers État*; and in this way it would not be possible for the first two orders to outvote the commons. To achieve this it would be necessary for the three estates to sit in a united assembly. The clergy and nobles had wished to deliberate separately and hoped by this means to deprive the commons of their power. This provoked a storm of opposition. The National party, led by such men as Talleyrand,

Mirabeau and the Abbé Sieyès—all of whom we shall meet later in an educational context—was organised to destroy existing abuses and to introduce a limited monarchy. 'What is the Third Estate?' asked Sieyès in one of his brochures. 'Everything. What is it in the political order? Nothing. What does it ask? To count for something.' It was not long (17 June 1789) before the Third Estate, joined now by many representatives of the clergy and some of the nobility, had declared themselves a National Assembly. In the face of opposition from the King this body set itself the task of drawing up a new constitution; and for this reason it is known henceforth as the Constituent Assembly.

The constitution was gradually hammered out between the years 1789 and 1791 amidst stormy debates and against a background of political upheavals and even scenes of violence and bloodshed. It was introduced by a Declaration of the Rights of Man and of the Citizen (26 August 1789). This proclaimed the sovereignty of the nation and the equality of its members in the eyes of the law; it enunciated freedom of opinion in speech and in the press; it asserted security of property and demanded a just distribution of taxation. But it said nothing specifically about education either as an individual right or as a State obligation. However, the fact that all citizens were conceded the right to 'take part personally or by their representatives' in the formation of laws, and that all offices of State, at whatever level, were to be equally accessible to those qualified to fill them, would seem to presuppose an educated populace in which the individual would have the opportunity of making the most of his ability and aptitude. When the new constitution was eventually promulgated it gave expression to the principles set

57

forth in the Declaration of Rights. It retained the monarchy as a mere figure-head, and instituted a single-chamber Assembly composed of deputies from the eighty-three departments[1] into which it had divided the country. In addition an article was inserted in the constitution (3 and 4 September 1791) to the effect that 'a system of public instruction shall be created, common to all citizens and gratuitous so far as that part of education is concerned which is necessary for all men alike. Schools of various grades shall be supplied as necessary over the whole kingdom'. The system was to be organised by the administrative units which had recently been set up.

The force of events had lent a particular significance to this article in the constitution. Although the writings of the *philosophes* and parliamentarians had aroused much interest in the question of popular education, the financial and other difficulties of the latter part of the eighteenth century had made it impossible for any definite action to be taken. Right up to the outbreak of the Revolution, therefore, education in France remained much as has been described in chapter 1, and at all levels it was still largely and ultimately under Church control. The existing provision, as has been shown, was

[1] By a decree of 14 December 1789 the old provinces were abolished and subsequently (15 January 1790) the departments were created. They were sub-divided into districts, and these in turn into cantons and communes—all of them administrative units having little relation to the central government. Paris also had administrative divisions called *arrondissements*. The cantons were suppressed by a decree of 26 June 1793, but were re-established by the Constitution of the Year VIII (1795). The Constitution of the Year VIII (1799) set up *arrondissements* which were like the old districts but bigger and fewer, and these deprived the cantons of their administrative functions. (See below p. 199.) Refer to F. Boursin and A. Challamel, *Dictionnaire de la Révolution française* (Paris, 1893): 'Départements', 'Districts' and 'Paris'.

not inconsiderable even if it were unco-ordinated and badly distributed. It would therefore have seemed a wise course for the Constituent Assembly to re-organise this and build on it a State system, such as had been recommended by reformers and in some of the *cahiers* and eventually in specific terms in the constitution itself. But instead of that it embarked on a scheme of destruction, in the hope apparently of being able to start afresh *ab initio*. A law of 4 August 1789 had swept away all seignorial exemptions and privileges. The dues known as *dîmes* were abolished. These were a form of tithe which for centuries had been one of the chief sources of revenue for Church-sponsored educational institutions. Not only that, but in February 1791 another source of revenue, the *octrois*—a form of indirect taxation— were also abolished. A good many schools and colleges, which were run by municipalities but often staffed by ecclesiastics, had to a greater or less extent benefited from these levies. The abolition of seignorial dues also impoverished many local magnates who had endowed or maintained schools and who were now unable to continue their subsidies. It seems, however, that the law of 4 August 1789 was not everywhere or fully or immediately applied as regards educational establishments; and there was a tendency, particularly in the case of schools run by municipalities, to postpone its operation pending the establishment of a new educational system. But, none the less, there is much evidence to show the distress and disorganisation caused by the withdrawal of these two sources of subsidy. Some colleges—e.g. those at Gap, Valence and Avignon—lost the whole of their revenues, and in many other cases resources were greatly reduced. Protests and petitions poured into the Assembly not only from teachers of

59

every degree, whether in universities, colleges or schools, but also from municipalities and other organisations which had educational responsibilities.

This blow to educational finance was serious enough but an even heavier one came in another form. In November 1789 the property of the Church had been nationalised and the admission of new members to religious orders prohibited. But the Church Establishment Act (*Constitution civile du Clergé*)[1] of July 1790 turned the Church of France into a State department and started a conflict between Church and State which was destined to persist, with varying intensity, for more than a century. Bishops and clergy were henceforth to be appointed by local election and paid a salary by the State. Moreover, all ecclesiastics were required to take an oath of allegiance to the constitution which had been decreed by the Assembly and accepted by the King. By a further decree of 22 March 1791 this requirement was extended to cover teachers, even if they were laymen. Thus not only were the universities, colleges and seminaries affected, but also the 'little schools' and the teaching congregations such as the Oratorians, Ursulines and Christian Brothers. Unless their members took the prescribed oath they were to be deprived of their functions, dismissed, and replaced by teachers who were 'assermentés'. This decree split the ranks of the teachers as the Civil Constitution had split those of the clergy; but in the event the majority of them at all levels refused to take a step which was condemned by the Pope and would imply a disloyalty to the Church. Moreover even in cases where they were prepared to do this parents were often unwilling to entrust their

[1] The text is given in J. M. Thompson, *French Revolution Documents* (Oxford, 1933), pp. 67–82.

children to schools run under the new conditions; and the result was that many of these were deserted.

The Constituent Assembly had a life of just over two years—from June 1789 to September 1791. During this period, as has been shown, it had practically destroyed the educational system of the country by the withdrawal of its sources of revenue and the imposition of the constitutional oath upon ecclesiastical and lay teachers alike. But national education continued to be a subject of interest, not only in the debates in the Assembly itself, but also in pamphlets and the press. One of the first proposals put forward was a *Mémoire sur l'éducation nationale française*, which was considered by the Constituent Assembly on 11 December 1790. The author, the Abbé Audrein, was a priest who had taken the civil oath and had been elected representative of the department of Morbihan. He was an out-and-out republican. For him the aim of education is 'to guarantee the stability of the constitution'. All schools are to be under State control. There is to be a system of primary and secondary schools, and parallel with them boarding establishments because 'the home is un-favourable to a good education'. No private establish-ments can therefore be allowed; 'whoever wishes to educate himself simply according to his own ideas is a bad citizen'. However, Audrein makes a concession to Protestant parents who will be allowed to send their children to national *pensionnats* in which the reformed religion is taught.

Two much more liberal and important projects also appeared during this period; and if the contemporary state of affairs had made it possible to give some effect to them the work of destruction might have been counteracted and the demand in the constitution itself for a system of public instruction might have been implemented. These projects were the work of the two statesmen Mirabeau and Talleyrand; and it remains now to consider their proposals in some detail.

Honoré Gabriel Riqueti, Comte de Mirabeau, as his title implies, was a member of the *noblesse*. After a stormy and somewhat disreputable youth he spent some time in Switzerland, Holland and England, and started upon a career as a writer. He attracted some attention as a pamphleteer on political and social subjects. But when the States-General was summoned in 1798 he was rejected as representative of the *noblesse* of Provence, and turned aside to become deputy of the *Tiers État* for Aix. He had an influential political career. He was no extremist, but sought to remodel the monarchy on constitutional lines, somewhat on the English pattern. In April 1791 he died, worn out by his youthful excesses and the hard work of his later years.

Among his papers found after his death were some projects for educational reform; and later in the year these documents, under the title of *Travail sur l'éducation publique*, were published by his friend J. G. Cabanis.[1] Mirabeau agrees in some measure with the criticisms which had been levelled at the educational system by many of the philosophical writers who had preceded him; but his scheme does not go very far and it represents a kind of transition between the

[1] It is only fair to say that the authorship of these documents has been questioned (see L. Liard, *L'Enseignement supérieur en France* (2 vols, Paris, 1882–94), I, 128, and Louis-Grimaud, *Histoire de la liberté d'enseignement en France* (4 vols, Grenoble, 1944), II, 57 n. and M. J. Guillaume, *Procés verbaux...de l'Assemblée législative* (Paris, 1889), p. vi, n. 3). They may have been largely the work of Cabanis himself, but at any rate they probably express Mirabeau's views. They are reprinted in Hippeau, *L'Instruction publique*, I, 1–32.

educational ideas and practice of the *Ancien Régime* and the more drastic and far-reaching proposals which were put forward during the subsequent years of the Revolution.

Mirabeau begins by asserting the need to restart society by a restitution of natural human rights; and the only way to achieve this is by means of a good system of public education. The government must therefore concern itself with this matter. What then should be the principles underlying educational reform? The first and perhaps the most important is that colleges and institutions of higher education should be under the sole control of the magistrates who truly represent the people because they have been elected by them. As to elementary education Mirabeau seems less enthusiastic. He says that where a parish school has been preserved from ruin a sum of 100 to 200 livres per annum should be assigned for its upkeep from the funds of the department in which it is situated. But the schoolmaster will also be authorised to receive fees from his pupils. Mirabeau decides against gratuitous education on the grounds that a master who receives fees will be more interested in improving his techniques, and the pupils more likely to value the teaching which they receive. Mirabeau does not entirely rule out the teaching congregations which give a free education, but he would employ them with caution. He tends to distrust their spirit of loyalty to their order, which may overrule their loyalty to the established government. These elementary schools are to teach reading, writing ciphering, and also if possible the drawing of plans and simple surveying. Like several other educational reformers of the period, Mirabeau lays stress on the importance of providing text-books which will give information about the republican constitution and explain the principles of political and personal morality. But as to curriculum and methods of instruction, these should not be prescribed by the Assembly. Such matters will be perfected by the general advance of knowledge and the indirect influence of the law. The schoolmaster himself is to be chosen by the director of the district from three candidates nominated by the canton in which the school is situated. Every school-master who distinguishes himself in his calling will receive rewards determined and distributed by the director of the department.

So much then for elementary education which apparently is not to be obligatory or gratuitous, and which is organised in a rather half-hearted fashion. Mirabeau shows greater interest when he deals with secondary and higher education. He adheres to the mainly classical curriculum of the *collèges* of the *Ancien Régime*. 'I am far from wishing to proscribe', he says, 'the study of the dead languages; on the contrary this should be encouraged.' He wishes in particular to revive 'that beautiful language, Greek, which has so perfect an analytic structure and so harmoniously achieves all the beauties of language'. This is a criticism of the contemporary Faculty of Arts where, in spite of Rollin, Greek had for long been neglected, although more attention had been given to it by the Jesuits and some of the other teaching orders. Mirabeau values the classical languages not only for the content of their literature, but also because they help one to appreciate and use one's own vernacular language. He believes, too, that Greek and Latin have a kind of psychological value because they are 'best fitted to furnish the most valuable theories as to the workings of the mind in the

64

expression of ideas'. At the same time he deprecates the use of Latin as a medium of instruction and says that all teaching should be given in French. In order to provide this secondary education based on the Classics Mirabeau claims that there should be at least one *collège*, giving this sort of instruction, in each department. Boys would be admitted at the age of ten and would give the first two years of their course mainly to Greek and Latin. This would correspond to the two 'Grammar' forms of the Faculty of Arts college. The next two stages deal mainly with poetry and rhetoric, and this is followed by a two-year course in philosophy. This course is also adopted from the customary practice of the *Ancien Régime*, and it contains nothing which is really original.

What is perhaps the most interesting feature of Mirabeau's scheme is his design for a National Lycée, situated in Paris—though even this has much in common with the Collège de France, which was one educational institution of the *Ancien Régime* which existed throughout the Revolution. The object of this establishment of higher education would be to procure for the élite of French youth the means of completing their education. A hundred students, sent from all the departments, would be maintained there at the expense of the nation and for a specified period. The teachers would include the most celebrated philosophers, scholars and scientists, 'selected by the unbiased vote of public opinion'. Their task would be not merely to teach but also to conduct research; and Mirabeau lays great stress on the need to establish general basic methods which underlie the art of directing the understanding in its search after truth, and the application of this in the various subjects of study. Thus the first chair

5   65   BEA

to be established in the National Lycée will be that of Method. Its occupant will explain the processes of reasoning and the mechanism of language or universal grammar. All this is reminiscent of Descartes and, after him, of the Port-Royalists. There will also be chairs of political economy and ethics, and two of universal history. Then come the sciences. A professor is assigned to each of the following: geometry and algebra, mechanics and hydraulics, general physics, physiology. Where necessary the occupant of the chair will be assisted by a demonstrator, and the necessary equipment for scientific study and research will also be provided. The chairs of languages will include one for Hebrew, one for Greek and one for Latin. There will also be one professor each for Turkish, Arabic and Persian, as well as for modern European languages such as Italian, Spanish, English and German. These teachers will not confine themselves to grammar and vocabulary, but in addition they will deal with the literature of the language which they profess. Mirabeau also emphasises the utility of a knowledge of modern foreign languages in reference to international commerce and diplomatic relations.

With regard to the education of women Mirabeau takes a view similar to that of Rousseau in his *Émile*. Men, who are destined to take part in affairs, should be educated in the public national system which has been described, but women are concerned with domestic life which is suited to their 'constitution délicate'. Their purpose is to perpetuate the race, to watch over the development of their children and to rule men by 'la puissance irrésistable de la faiblesse'. Their amiable qualities are developed in the bosom of the family and they should not leave home except in special circumstances. Mirabeau does not demand the suppression of the convents in which so many of the girls of his day were educated, but he seems to wish that, though they may be conducted by 'associations libres', they should none the less be subject to some sort of control by public authorities. As regards elementary education, he would preserve any existing schools which give instruction for girls in reading, writing and arithmetic, and he would provide more schools of this kind in areas where they do not exist.

This then is the scheme with which Mirabeau proposes to replace the educational system which the Constituent Assembly had abolished. 'In order to reconstruct everything', he says, 'it was necessary to destroy everything.' But the new constitution will breathe new life into the dry bones; and this can be done only by 'un bon système d'éducation publique', which will complete the work of regeneration and base the well-being of the people on its virtues, and its virtues on its enlightenment. All this is set forth with a truly Gallic eloquence; but the continued disorder and disorganisation (including the King's flight to Varennes and the threat of armed intervention from outside to support the monarchy in France), which followed Mirabeau's death, made the institution of a State educational system as far off as ever. His project was never laid before the Constituent Assembly or debated by it; but that did not mean that it had lost all interest in educational matters—as, indeed, is illustrated by the report submitted to it by Talleyrand. This therefore must now be described.

5-2

5   *Talleyrand's report*

Charles Maurice Talleyrand-Perigord was born in 1754. He was educated at the Collège d'Harcourt in the University of Paris and at the seminary of St Sulpice. He was ordained to the priesthood in 1778. However, he became increasingly critical of the social and political ideas of the *Ancien Régime* and of the claims of the Church. In 1780 he was appointed agent-general of the clergy of France, a position which implied important administrative duties in the relations between the clergy and the civil power. In 1789, in spite of his 'advanced' views, he was consecrated bishop of Autun. When therefore the States-General was convoked one of his first actions was to draw up a statement of the reforms which he wished it to carry out. He advocated a curtailment of seignorial privileges and an extension of local government, as well as legal and judicial reforms. His views were adopted by the clergy of his diocese and were embodied in the *cahier* which they submitted to the States-General. Talleyrand himself was chosen as their representative. He was one of four, out of thirty, bishops in the Assembly who took the oath of obedience to the Civil Constitution of the Clergy. In January 1791 he resigned from his see and two months later was condemned by the Pope.

In connection with the educational provisions which were added to the 1791 constitution, a committee of public instruction had been appointed, and it was on behalf of this body that Talleyrand presented his report.[1] It was considered by the Constituent Assembly

[1] Reprinted in Hippeau, *L'Instruction publique*, I, 33–184.

68

on 10, 11 and 19 September 1791; but by this time, as its work of constitution making was finished, it was on the point of dissolving itself. The suggestion was therefore made that a discussion of Talleyrand's proposals should be postponed until the new Assembly was convened; but he stressed the extreme urgency of the existing situation. 'Everywhere', he said, 'the universities have suspended their activities; the colleges are without discipline, without teachers, without pupils. It is necessary that things should be put right before the month of October.' However, the Constituent Assembly met for the last time on 30 September without taking any action on Talleyrand's report, though it decreed that this document, which is of considerable length, should be printed and referred to its successor, the Legislative Assembly.

The report lacks something of Mirabeau's rhetorical eloquence but it is much more closely argued. The first part of it consists of a discussion of general principles. The old methods in instruction are too monastic and they are not based on reason; the new constitution will acquire a new type of education. Law under the republican régime is—as it should be—the expression of the general will; but in order that it may be safeguarded from irresponsible and misguided attacks 'it is necessary that public reason, armed with the power that instruction and enlightenment can give, should continually forestall and repress such usurpations on the part of individuals'. Education is indeed a guarantee of freedom. The ignorant man is always at the mercy of those who have been better instructed; and if the new constitution is to be made really effective it must be understood and put into practice by citizens who have been educated. Moreover, education

is the chief means of ensuring progress and 'perfectibility', both for the individual and for society. It helps
men to realise their greatest potentialities, to make
full use of their rights and to respect and carry out
their duties as citizens. 'Instruction can be regarded
as a product of society, as a source of benefit to society
and equally as a fruitful source of benefits to the
individual.'

All this means that a general education should be
made available for everyone—not merely for the young
or for the male sex only, but for all ages and for women
as well as men. At the same time it is most important to
find the right persons for educational work, and all
kinds of talent can be appropriately utilised to compete
for the public esteem which will be their reward.
Society should encourage educational effort and facilitate all methods of teaching, while at the same time
protecting especially those whose real and immediate
usefulness is generally recognised and is directed
particularly to the support of the constitution and the
development of patriotic feeling. 'If everyone has the
right to receive the benefits of instruction, everyone has
the right to take part in disseminating it; for it is from
the competition of individual efforts that the greatest
good always results.' In a document entitled *Observations sur le rapport de Talleyrand* (1791) the 'maîtres de
pension de Paris' put forward certain criticisms, though
they accept much of what is recommended. They agree
that private schools should be required to give an
education which is 'conformé à la constitution'; but
anyone who so desires should be free to exercise the
functions of a teacher, subject to supervision by official
inspectors who will visit such schools at least once a
month. They will ensure that the teaching, accommoda-

tion, time-table, etc. are satisfactory. In this way it was hoped that 'the sacred rights of liberty would be neither assailed nor infringed'. In order to justify themselves private teachers and *maîtres de pension* would be willing to announce that the principal aim of their instruction was to teach republicanism. For example, 'All decrees emanating from this august senate, and especially the Rights of Man and the constitution will be analysed, justified, explained and adapted to the understanding of the pupils.'[1]

The educational system according to Talleyrand's plan can be classified in the usual three stages—primary, secondary and higher. Primary instruction should be available for everybody and there should be a primary school in every canton; but for a large number of pupils a type of education should be provided which will ensure a wider development of faculties and help the individual towards a more specialised career. To this end every district should have a secondary school. For a smaller élite institutions of higher education, one in each department, will provide further and professional instruction. Does this mean that education will be afforded gratuitously to everyone? Talleyrand, re-echoing the principle laid down in the constitution itself, replies that only that type of instruction should be free which is necessarily common to everybody—the elements which are indispensable to everyone whatever career he eventually takes up. But the education given in the district and department schools is not to be common to all, even though it is accessible to all who can profit by it. Although society should provide such

---

[1] *Petites Affiches*, November 1790; quoted by E. and J. de Goncourt, *Histoire de la société française pendant la Révolution* (Paris, 1854), p. 389.

institutions it does not follow that the principle of gratuity should apply here. 'Since those who attend these schools will reap real benefit from them it is perfectly fair that they should pay part of the cost and that they should contribute towards the means of providing for their teachers a competency which will lighten their labours.' However, at every stage ample scholarships and prizes will be made available, and in this way provision will be ensured for the educational needs of everyone. At each stage also the administration of educational institutions will be linked up with the different levels in the general administrative hierarchy of the State; and above them all and controlling them all will be the legislative body of the nation, invested with the power of the public will. This will act through six commissioners appointed by the King, and they will have the duty of making an annual report to the Assembly.

Talleyrand proceeds to sketch out a scheme of public instruction which is more detailed and more fully organised than Mirabeau's proposals. Up to the age of six or seven the child should be brought up in the family and receive a domestic education, for 'each family is a primary school and the father is its head'. The cantonal schools will provide instruction in the mother-tongue, both written and spoken, because the fundamental need in society is the communication of ideas and feelings. Talleyrand is anxious to eliminate patois (which he calls 'dialectes corrumpues'), because —in common with some other revolutionary thinkers— he feels that linguistic differences tend to emphasise class distinctions and militate against national unity as well as social and political equality.[1] Arithmetic, of

[1] On the revolution's attitude to patois see Fortescue, F 492 and F 493 (see Bibliographical Appendix, p. 257). See also below,

course, is necessary and its practical applications, as in the measurement of fields and buildings, should also be taught. To this can be added some elementary geography and history. As an ex-bishop, if not a very orthodox one, Talleyrand would have the primary school teach the elements of religion and the principles of morality. It is also necessary to instil a knowledge of the constitution, for one cannot too early make children acquainted with the régime under which they have to live and which, when they grow up, they must be prepared to defend even at the peril of their lives. Physical education is no less important than intellectual instruction; it will be imparted through exercises designed to promote health, to preserve and strengthen the body, and to inure it to manual work at a later stage. Children, whatever their status, must be made to realise that work is the basis of everything. Such then is the curriculum of the cantonal primary school.

The next stage is the district school the work of which will be the natural sequence and development of the instruction given in the primary school. The basic principles of the mother-tongue, which have been acquired there, will lead on to a more detailed study of the art of composition; and this will be reinforced by the acquirement of those ancient languages which enshrine the most valuable achievements of the human mind. Talleyrand also believes that the secondary school curriculum should include those modern languages which local or national conditions appear to render most useful. To the elements of religion acquired in the primary school we shall now add the history of

p. 130. One of the reasons for abolishing the old provinces, with their local dialects and traditions, and for substituting a system of departments was to counteract local loyalties and foster a feeling of nationhood and patriotism.

73

this subject and the explanation of the grounds upon which religious faith is based. In the same way matters of personal and political morality should be dealt with in greater detail. The Declaration of the Rights of Man and of the Citizen will be the basis of this instruction. Talleyrand wishes the secondary school curriculum to be organised not by classes, as was customary in the *collèges*, but by courses. This would have resulted in an incoherent and unco-ordinated system which might have been difficult to administer, and—as we shall see later in the case of the central schools—it tends to prove ineffective in practice. It might also encourage premature specialisation.

The departmental schools of higher education are designed to provide varied courses for those careers which necessitate professional training, and 'in the exercise of which mistakes will have serious consequences for society—for example, the ministry of the Church, the practice of law, of surgery, and of the military art'. Talleyrand devotes a large part of his report to these institutions. There will be seminaries for the training of ordinands in the Catholic Church, and these will be situated in cathedral cities under the eye of the bishop. The students will be instructed not only in matters of faith and religion, but also in the duties of administering a parish and in the art of preaching. The schools of medicine will teach the basic sciences and their application to the art of healing; but the ultimate aim should always be a practical one, and for this reason every medical school should be associated with a teaching hospital where there will be ample opportunity for clinical experience. The qualifying examinations for medical students should be rigorous; but Talleyrand does not envisage any form of medical

74

register. He wishes doctors to be judged by their works and not by their certificates. 'One should be able to be admitted a doctor without having attended a medical school, and one might have attended one without becoming qualified. Thus would be achieved that which justice requires, liberty demands, and the welfare of the public necessitates.' There seems to be some inconsistency here.

Talleyrand goes on to discuss the teaching of law. The new revolutionary régime implies a new legal system. The fundamental study will therefore be that of the public national law as laid down in the constitution and the acts which have been developed from it. Canon law can be disregarded; but the future advocate must be made familiar with the forms of legal procedure. The course should not be too rigorously organised, but—as with medicine—the qualifying tests should ensure the effectiveness of the candidates. Talleyrand considers that ten schools of law will be sufficient to meet the needs of the country.

He deals next with institutions for training military officers, and here he takes as his pattern the military schools which had already been set up in various parts of France during the reign of Louis XIV.[1] There are, he says, twenty-three military divisions in the country and there should be a professional school in each of them. Candidates will be admitted from the district schools at the age of not under fourteen and not over sixteen. The course will last four years and will include not only military subjects, but also English and German, drawing, mathematics applied to the art of war, as well as geography, history, and a study of the constitution.

[1] Refer to Vallet de Viriville, *Histoire de l'instruction publique* (Paris, 1849), pp. 265–7.

The training will inculcate social and political morality, patriotism, love of liberty, and discipline. 'Our military schools will train men who will at once be free citizens and obedient soldiers—and, as a result, good leaders.' In addition to the twenty-three schools there will be six special academies placed on the frontiers of the kingdom at Lille, Metz, Strasbourg, Besançon, Grenoble and Perpignan; and these will be mainly concerned with the practical side of military instruction. Special scholarships to be held in these academies will be available for selected candidates sent from the departments, and preference will be given to the children of ex-soldiers—especially if they are orphans. Other students may come from the divisional schools and these will be chosen by competitive examination. These military academies will be organised on regimental lines and commanded by retired officers. In all this preoccupation with military training one may perhaps sense the current uneasiness as to a threat of war from Austria and Prussia, following on the King's flight to Varennes and the Declaration of Pilnitz.

At the summit of the educational system Talleyrand envisages a National Institute which, like Mirabeau's Lycée National, will be a kind of 'Solomon's House'. 'It includes everything and perfects everything.' It will provide higher education in all branches of science and arts alike—'tout ce que le génie peut atteindre'. It will be situated in Paris and will be equipped with all the resources which libraries, laboratories, art galleries, and museums can provide. In describing this Institute Talleyrand lets his imagination run riot; but his project is an interesting comment on the advance, made by thinkers of the latter part of the eighteenth century, on the aims and curriculum of the contemporary universities—or even of the Collège de France itself. Not only are chairs provided for the usual scientific and literary subjects, but there are also to be professors of painting, sculpture, architecture, music, agriculture, and veterinary science, while the section devoted to medicine includes pharmacy and first-aid.

Talleyrand goes on to stress the necessity for establishing a library in each of the eighty-three departments. They will be formed largely from the collections of books which belonged to monasteries; these had been despoiled and largely destroyed[1] by the decree of 2 November 1789 which nationalised Church property. Talleyrand estimates that no less than 4,194,412 such volumes are available. Some of course are valueless and in some cases the copies are duplicated; but there will remain a nucleus which has been selected and this will be added to year by year. The existing Bibliothèque du Roi at Paris will remain as it is; 'we should try to perfect it, but it would be unreasonable to alter or destroy it'.

Finally Talleyrand deals with the education of women, and into this matter he goes rather more deeply than did Mirabeau. He realises that it is bound up with the question of civil rights. Half the human race is excluded by the other half from any share in the duties of government, even though women may be owners of property. On the other hand our aim should be the greatest happiness of the greatest number. If the exclusion of women from public life and their concentration upon domestic duties is really a means of increasing the mutual happiness of the two sexes, then the existing situation should be recognised and sanc-

[1] See E. and J. de Goncourt, *Histoire de la société française pendant la Révolution*, pp. 367–71.

tioned by society. So in the end Talleyrand takes up the conventional point of view. 'Is it not obvious that harmonious division of powers has been, as it were, set forth and revealed by nature in assigning to the two sexes functions which are so evidently distinct?...Do not make rivals of your companions in life; do not interfere with a union which no other interest or competition should break.' Even if women renounce any political rights, they can rest assured that the law will confirm and even increase their civil rights.

However, if they are to be thus assured they must be helped to understand their position by means of education. But it should begin in the home. As far as schools for girls are concerned, before the abolition of monastic vows these were provided in large numbers by the various teaching orders of women. The education which they gave can be criticised on many grounds, but they did at any rate 'offer a retreat for innocence'. We should therefore seek to establish in their stead other institutions which will compensate for their destruction. Each department should provide a sufficient number of schools for girls, staffed by women who will not take vows but whose integrity will ensure public confidence. Up to the age of eight girls can attend co-educational primary schools and follow the course of instruction which they give; but at the end of childhood they should remain in the family dwelling, and it must never be forgotten that boarding establishments, such as were the old convent schools, are no real substitute for home-life. At the same time, where it is necessary for a girl to enter on an apprenticeship to some suitable occupation, 'maisons retirées', under departmental inspection, will provide an elementary technical education.

Talleyrand's educational proposals obviously have much in common with those of Mirabeau, though they take us rather further. They have been criticised on several grounds—e.g. that they give no indication as to how the educational system is to be financed or how teachers are to be recruited and trained. It might also have been unwise to tie the provision of educational institutions too rigidly to the administrative organisation which the Constitutent Assembly had devised. For example, the needs of a thinly populated area might be different from those where a large number of children had to be catered for. If the primary school is to be without exception located in the chief town of a canton, it might be difficult for children in a scattered country district to attend it. There might again be disadvantages in centralising the highest ranges of education in Paris, instead of preserving a system of provincial universities such as had been in existence under the *Ancien Régime*. But taken as a whole Talleyrand's scheme is a very progressive one. Although in its main outlines it has been realised under modern conditions, it represented a great advance at the time when it was put forward.

6 The Legislative Assembly. Condorcet's report. The education of women

The Constituent Assembly held its last session on 30 September 1791, and on the next day its successor, the Legislative Assembly, met for the first time. In this body, which had been set up under the new constitution, the clergy and nobility no longer had separate representation, but it consisted of 745 deputies who had been elected on a fairly wide property franchise; however, owing to the exaction of the civil oath from the voters and the complicated system of voting, many of those who were qualified to go to the polls failed to exercise their right; and the Constituent Assembly, by a self-denying ordinance, had already decreed that none of its members should be eligible as candidates for the new Assembly. Like most elected bodies, this soon divided itself into parties. It comprised the Feuillants who advocated a constitutional monarchy, the Girondins who were moderate republicans, and the extremist Jacobins who were led by Robespierre. The Legislative Assembly had a stormy career of just under a year; this was marked by dissension among the parties, the attack on the monarchy and the declaration of war against Austria. To this country many of the nobility had emigrated after the abolition of their order in June 1790, and they were suspected of plotting against the revolutionary government of their native land. But in spite of tensions and dissensions the Assembly did not altogether disregard educational matters. It certainly took no definite action on Talleyrand's report which had been bequeathed to it in printed form by the

Constituent Assembly; but one of its first actions was to appoint a Committee of Public Instruction composed of twenty-four members. Its president, Louis-François-Antoine Arbogast, was a mathematician and represented the department of Bas-Rhin. In December 1791 this body started an inquiry into the state of primary education in France; but the replies to its investigations seem to have been lost or destroyed, and little is known about them.[1] On 20 and 21 April 1792, however, one of its members, the Marquis de Condorcet, presented a report[2] and the project of a law which once again sketched out a scheme for a national system of education.

Marie-Jean-Antoine-Nicholas Caritat, Marquis de Condorcet, belonged to a noble and ancient family of Picardy, and had been educated by the Jesuits and at the Collège de Navarre in the University of Paris. He had attained distinction as a mathematician and in 1773 was elected secretary of the Academy of Sciences. He wrote a number of mathematical treatises and also lives of Turgot and Voltaire; and he showed a deep and active concern for political and educational matters. Indeed, as recently as 1790 he had published five *Mémoires sur l'instruction publique*. He was elected to represent the City of Paris in the Legislative Assembly, and in view of his experience and interest it was appropriate that he should be chosen as a member of its Committee of Public Instruction. It was in this capacity that he sponsored its educational project.

Condorcet begins his report by emphasising the fundamental importance of a national system of

[1] See however Louis-Grimaud, *Histoire de la liberté d'enseignement en France*, II, 38–9.
[2] Reprinted in Guillaume, *Procès-verbaux du Comité d'Instruction Publique de l'Assemblée Législative* (Paris, 1889), pp. 188–226, and in Hippeau, *L'Instruction publique*, I, 185–288.

education in order to realise true liberty and political equality. 'To afford all members of the human race the means of providing for their needs, of securing their welfare, of recognising and exercising their rights, of understanding and fulfilling their duties; to assure for everyone opportunities of perfecting their skill and rendering themselves capable of the social duties to which they have a right to be called; to develop to the utmost the talents with which nature has endowed them and, in so doing, to establish among all citizens a true equality and thus make real the political equality realised by the law—this should be the primary aim of a national system of education, and from this point of view its establishment is for the public authority an obligation of justice.' Such a system will increase individual happiness and the prosperity of all alike, and so contribute in each generation to the general perfecting of the human race. This is a huge task, but as a step towards the creation of a new educational system Condorcet proposes to discuss in particular the distribution and general organisation of institutions of public instruction. The scheme should be such as will ensure that all citizens equally shall receive the instruction which can be given to all alike, but at the same time no section of the community shall be debarred from receiving the more advanced type of education which is not possible for everybody.

As a convinced supporter of republican government, Condorcet advocates freeing public education from the influence of the Crown by constituting an autonomous teaching body which will ensure the inculcation of republican ideals; but at the same time in order that educational institutions may be at liberty to teach the truth it is important that they should be as free as possible from political control. As their independence cannot be absolute, they should be dependent solely on the Assembly of Representatives of the People which, of all political bodies, is least liable to corruption, least likely to be affected by private interest, most amenable to the influence of enlightened men, and least inimical to progress. In spite of his definite political views Condorcet is no advocate for using the school as an agent for propaganda. 'No public body', he says, 'should have the authority or the influence to prevent the development of new truths, or the teaching of theories contrary to its own political views or its current interests.' In a previous memorandum Condorcet had referred to the law of 1698 which was re-enacted in 1724[1] and which required Protestant parents to send their children to Catholic schools. Such an action, he says, deprives the father of a natural right which is anterior to any man-made law. It is for reasons like this also that Condorcet believes that independent schools should be permitted to exist alongside of those provided by the State. 'Private schools', he says, 'are a means of correcting the defects of public instruction and of maintaining the zeal of teachers through the spirit of competition...If any citizen is allowed to open an educational establishment the result will be that the State schools will be absolutely compelled to keep themselves at least up to the level of the private schools.'

Condorcet takes a wide view of education. It should not cease the moment one leaves school. There is no age when learning is useless or no longer possible; and it is all the more necessary in cases where education during childhood has been restricted within narrow

---

[1] See above, p. 2.

6-2

limits. Henceforth, whatever the social position of the citizen or his parents, instruction to the very limits of his ability should be available. 'If nature has given you talents you can develop them and they will not be lost either for yourself or your country.' Thus education should be universal and equally shared so far as is possible within the limits imposed by its cost, the distribution of the population, and the shorter or longer period which children can give to it. In its different stages it should comprise the entire range of human knowledge and ensure to all, of whatever age, the opportunity of preserving knowledge and of extending it.

After having thus established his general principles Condorcet proceeds to discuss in detail the organisation of the system which he proposes. He extends somewhat the schemes of Mirabeau and Talleyrand, and would have five degrees of instruction to which he gives the names of primary schools, secondary schools, institutes, *lycées*, and the National Society of Sciences and Arts.

(1) *Primary schools.* Here the individual will be taught how to conduct himself and how to enjoy his rights to the full. There will be a school of this type with one teacher in every village of at least 400 inhabitants. The subjects taught will be reading and writing (which presupposes some elementary notions of grammar); simple arithmetic and land measurement; some knowledge of the agricultural and industrial products of the school region; and the basic ideas of morality and the rules of conduct which derive from them, as well as the laws of the nation so far as they can be understood by children. The Declaration of the Rights of Man and the details of the French constitution are not to be presented as if—like the Ten Commandments

—they were tables handed down from heaven, but as founded upon simple principles dictated by reason.

The primary-school course will last for four years and children will normally enter upon it at the age of six. But the primary-school teacher will not confine himself to this work. Every Sunday he will hold a conference attended by citizens of all ages. 'By continuing instruction in this way throughout life we shall prevent the knowledge acquired at school from being forgotten too soon. We shall keep minds usefully active. We shall give people information about new legislation, new agricultural or economic methods about which it is important to have information. They can also be taught the art of self-instruction—as, for instance, looking up a word in a dictionary, consulting an index, tracing out information on a map or a diagram, making notes or extracts.' In order to assist instruction in the primary school Condorcet, like La Chalotais, thinks that elementary text-books should be prepared, whether for adults or children, which they can read for themselves and which will make learning pleasant and easy. Such works will be composed as the result of a competition open to all citizens who are willing and able to contribute in this way to the cause of public instruction. Not only this, but treatises will also be written for the benefit of teachers, so that they may know how to apply educational principles and adapt their methods to the aptitudes of their pupils. If it is felt that present conditions make it necessary to restrict primary education within too narrow limits, it will be easy to extend these when the opportunity arrives as the result of the general improvement of the people, the more equitable distribution of incomes, and the progress made in methods of teaching. The ultimate reduction of the national debt and of unnecessary expenditure will also make it possible to devote a larger proportion of the public revenues to really useful purposes.

(2) *Secondary schools*. These will be designed for children from families who can dispense with their work for a longer time and thus allow them a greater number of years for their education or enable them to take it to a more advanced degree. They are, in fact, an equivalent of what afterwards became known as 'higher primary schools'. Each district and each town of four thousand inhabitants will have a school of this type. The course of study in all such schools will be the same, but they will have one, two or three teachers, according to the number of pupils who may be expected to attend them. The basis of their instruction will comprise some knowledge of mathematics, of natural history and of applied chemistry, and a more advanced study of ethics and social science, together with elementary instruction in commerce—in short, a technical curriculum. As in the primary school, the teachers will give weekly lectures open to all citizens. Every school will have its own library and a small collection of meteorological instruments, models of machines, and natural history specimens. The collections will doubtless be augmented from time to time by gifts and exchanges. If in rural areas the inhabitants are too poor to send their children away to attend a secondary school, there are at any rate certain periods of the year when they are not busy and when time could be given to voluntary study. On the other hand, those who are destined to become craftsmen and are serving their apprenticeship in the neighbouring towns will receive in the secondary schools that type of instruction which they will most need.

86

'In this way equality is once more preserved, rather than destroyed, by the establishment of secondary schools. The farmer in the country, the workman in the town, will not disdain study once they have realised its advantages, either from their own experience or from that of others.' To encourage this type of adult education the Sunday courses will be repeated each year or perhaps every other year, so that the instruction given will be thoroughly understood and never forgotten. Additional information on new methods and discoveries will excite curiosity and increase interest.

(3) *Institutes*. There will be 110 of these establishments, distributed over the country as follows: sixty-one departments will have one each, nineteen two each, two three each, and Paris itself five. In these institutions will be taught whatever knowledge is useful to the citizen, no matter for what profession he is intended. Condorcet gives as examples agriculture, the mechanical arts, the military art, even the elementary medical knowledge needed by the general practitioner, the midwife and the veterinary surgeon. It is in the institutes also that the masters in the secondary schools will be trained and where teachers for primary schools, who have already been educated in schools of the second degree, will take their course of professional training. Condorcet points out the difficulty of classifying the various branches of human knowledge into hard and fast 'subjects'; but his predilection for scientific studies is very evident and he reacts strongly against the classical and scholastic curriculum of the Faculty of Arts and the Jesuit colleges. 'No doubt,' he says, 'in applying oneself to literature, grammar, history, politics and philosophy, one can achieve precision

methods and a sound knowledge of logic, and yet be totally ignorant of the natural sciences'—a criticism which even today has not wholly lost its point. An elementary study of literary subjects may make use of the reason, but they do not develop it. The sciences are a remedy against prejudice and narrowness of mind and are of use in all walks of life. The same arguments were repeated seventy years later by Herbert Spencer. Condorcet believes that there is in contemporary Europe a general intellectual movement in favour of scientific study[1] and that this is the key to improvements in the social order.

He goes on to consider the place of language teaching in the curriculum. Under the *Ancien Régime* the colleges gave a six-years' course based on the study of Latin. 'But in view of the time available, by what strange privilege should Latin be made the most important subject of study?' There is no really important work on science or philosophy or politics which has not been translated; and the facts which such books contain can be found better developed and amplified with new information in works which have been written in the vulgar tongue. The Classics are full of errors, and we are trying to teach the truth and train the reason. In studying them therefore one has to be continually on one's guard.

The instruction given in the institutes will be divided into courses, and it will be possible for a student to follow as many as four of them at the same time, or to take them part-time. A brilliant pupil may be able to compass 'la totalité de l'instruction' during his five-year course; but one who has 'des dispositions moins heureuses' will devote himself only to such parts of the curriculum as especially appeal to him. 'Thus the various arrangements will accommodate themselves to differences of ability or to individual needs.' Once a month the professors will deliver lectures which deal mainly with scientific discoveries and experiments, and their application in industry. As in the primary and secondary schools, so also in the institutes, specially prepared text-books will be used. But in this case the authors will not be selected by competition, but will be appointed. It is to be hoped that men of real distinction in the various branches of science will be willing to co-operate in this work. Each institute will have its library, museum and botanical garden, and these will be placed under the care of a curator. Demonstrations, discussions, even examinations will be arranged; but 'in every class-room a place should be reserved for those who are not pupils and are therefore not liable to be questioned or given tasks to do, but who wish to follow a course of instruction'. In garrison towns special attention will be given to the military art and in seaports courses in navigation will be provided. Ethical training in the institutes will be based on reason, but religious teaching will be excluded. 'The Constitution, by recognising the right of every individual to choose his religion, and by establishing complete equality among all the inhabitants of France, utterly forbids the introduction into public education of any teaching which, by excluding the children of some citizens, would destroy the equality of social advantages and give to particular doctrines a preference which is contrary to the liberty of opinions. It is therefore absolutely necessary to separate ethics from the principles of any particular religion, and not to allow in public instruction the teaching of any religious creed.'

(4) *Lycées*. These are of university standard and there will be nine of them situated in various parts of France. One should be situated in Paris, but the others preferably in smaller towns where the cost of living is moderate and where business or industrial interests will not stifle intellectual pursuits. In these *lycées* all branches of knowledge will be taught to their fullest extent. Here will be trained those scholars who make intellectual culture and the perfecting of their intellectual faculties one of the chief aims in life, as will also those who are proposing to follow one of the professions in which success can be obtained only by a profound study of one or more of the sciences. The teachers for the institutes will be trained in the *lycées*. The instruction provided here will be more extensive than exists in any similar institutions in other European countries, and for this reason it may be hoped that they will attract students from abroad—a fact which will at once be advantageous to commerce and will also tend to promote international understanding. The *lycées* will give instruction in all the more important foreign languages, and even the ancient ones. At this stage young people whose minds are already trained can study these latter subjects without danger 'because they will be capable of estimating the results of a difference of moral values, methods of government and language'. They will realise the progress which has been made in opinion and ideas, and at the same time they will be able to appreciate and evaluate the beauty of their models. Instruction in *lycées* will be open to young people who are completing their education, and also to interested adults.

At each of the four stages of instruction already described tuition will be absolutely free. 'The advantage of education, when it is no longer associated with wealth, will be less obvious and consequently less dangerous to equality. The advantage of having been born wealthy will be counterbalanced by the equal, and even superior, intellectual standard achieved by those who have an additional incentive for acquiring it.' This implies also that there must be standard rates of pay for teachers, so that they may not be in any way dependent upon fees, and it may not be possible for prosperous towns and rich agricultural areas to attract the most competent candidates. There will also be less danger of rivalry between educational institutions, with teachers trying to show off and impress rather than instruct.

But though education is to be free, above the primary stage it ceases to be universal. Here we have the problem of selection for secondary education. We shall endeavour to secure for the country all the abilities which can be of service to it, and also to deprive no single individual of the opportunity of developing the abilities which he possesses. No exact details are given as to how the test is to be made, but children who have shown most promise at one stage of instruction will be entitled to proceed to the next stage and to be maintained, as well as taught, at public expense. They will be called 'State scholars' (*élèves de la patrie*). According to Condorcet's estimate they would number about 3850, of whom 1000 would be advanced enough to attend courses in the institutes and 600 in the *lycées*. Each year about 400 would come out and would then take up useful employments in society or devote themselves to scientific study.

(5) *The National Society of Sciences and Arts*. Like Mirabeau and Talleyrand, Condorcet envisages an institution at the summit of the whole educational

system which will supervise and direct it, and concern itself with the advancement of the sciences and the arts by collecting, encouraging and applying useful discoveries. 'It is no longer a question of educating children or even adults, but of the instruction of the people as a whole and the general perfecting of human reason.' This Society will comprise four sections which will hold their meetings separately and normally an individual can be a member of only one section at a time, though there will be no objection to members of one group attending meetings of another as visitors, if they wish to do so. In fact the meetings will also be open to interested members of the general public. The first section deals with the mathematical and physical sciences; the second with the moral and political sciences; the third with applied mathematics and physics—and this would include the mechanical arts, agriculture, navigation and medicine. The fourth section concerns itself with grammar, literature, the fine arts and erudition; but the fine arts, like the mechanical arts, should be considered in relation to the theory which underlies them. 'The object is to fill the gap between abstract science and the practice of it, between the principles of an art and its expression.'

The number of members of the National Society will be fixed. Half of them will reside normally in the departments, and this will ensure the advantage of spreading information more uniformly and placing it within the reach of a greater number of citizens. Once the National Society has been founded and composed of the most distinguished savants of the day, it will be recruited by co-option. A list of candidates will be drawn up and all the members of the various sections will vote on it; then the section directly concerned will make the final choice. In a similar way the various sections of the National Society will select those professors for the *lycées* with whose subjects they are concerned. Short lists of candidates for teaching posts in secondary and primary schools will be drawn up by the teachers in the institutes in each department. In the case of the secondary schools the final selection will be made by the municipal council of the area in which the school is situated; and in the primary schools by a meeting of fathers of families in the school's canton—as had been customary under the *Ancien Régime*. The inspection of primary and secondary schools will be carried out by a board composed of four members from the staff of the regional institute. A similar board from the *lycée* will inspect the institutes in its neighbourhood; and each section of the National Society will nominate every year three representatives to serve on a committee which will meet on fixed days to discuss problems concerned with the administration of *lycées*. It will also concern itself with improvements in educational methods. In this way, then, the whole educational hierarchy is elaborately organised and co-ordinated. The whole scheme implies a high degree of 'academic freedom'.

As regards the education of women Condorcet says definitely that instruction should be the same for both sexes alike. 'Since all instruction is limited to making truths known and explaining the proofs, it is difficult to see why a difference of sex should imply a choice among those truths or the methods of proving them.' So women will at any rate follow the earlier stages of instruction without being debarred from the higher ones if they have the ability to tackle them. Condorcet certainly says that if some professions are reserved

93

exclusively for men, women would not be admitted to the instruction which prepares specifically for them; but he sees no reason to debar them from a study of the sciences, and he believes that many of them will be able to make useful observations and experiments, and that they may even be better fitted than men to prepare elementary text-books for the use of children. Women, therefore, should share the instruction given to men, and that for several reasons. It will help them to supervise the education of their children. If they lacked instruction this would introduce into families an inequality which would militate against domestic happiness. Again, 'men who have profited by public instruction will more easily preserve its advantages if they find an approximately equal degree of education in their wives, and if they can share with them the reading which will keep this knowledge alive'. Finally, women have the same rights as men—and therefore the right to public instruction.

All this means that co-education is indicated at every stage and that it can be entrusted to a teacher of either sex. Condorcet points out that even at the university level in Italy women have held chairs with distinction. Moreover, co-education is economical, especially at the primary stage, for it would be difficult in rural areas particularly to have two one-sex schools in the same village. Condorcet advocates co-education also because he believes that, far from being dangerous to morality, it in fact conduces to it, because everything is open and under the eye of the teacher; and besides it promotes a friendly form of emulation, and not the selfish kind which is found in one-sex *collèges*. 'It may be feared', says Condorcet, 'that young people may be too much distracted from their school-work if they are concerned with more sentimental interests; but this fear is ill-founded. If this really is a danger it will be more than counterbalanced by the emulation inspired by the desire to merit the esteem of the person beloved ...The habit of wanting to be first is either stupid or unfortunate for anyone who has acquired it; and it is a real disaster for those who live in contact with such a person. But the habit of wanting to deserve esteem conduces to that inward peace which alone makes happiness possible and virtue easily attainable.' Perhaps it is at this point that Condorcet allows his imagination to get the better of his usual good sense.

The education of girls is dealt with in several of the reports presented to the Revolutionary assemblies, though it was not until the Guizot law of 1833 that a detailed system of primary instruction was provided for girls. So far as secondary education was concerned they had to wait until the Camille Sée reforms of 1880. But in addition to the plans for female education in such reports as those of Mirabeau, Talleyrand and Condorcet, there were one or two special projects dealing with this subject. If one may be allowed to anticipate a little, perhaps a reference may be made to them here. For example, the matter was raised by Jean-Marie Calès, deputy for Haute-Garonne, in July 1793. He says that there used to be numerous girls' schools run by teaching congregations, but the Revolution has suppressed these. He does not regret their disappearance, but they must be replaced. There is a need for 'maisons d'éducation confiées à des citoyennes connues par leurs vertus, leurs talents et leur amour pour les lois de l'État'. There will be no religious teaching and no frivolity. The 'art des toilettes' will disappear and affectation will give place to becoming modesty. 'The wife of a

95

republican, proud of the charms which her sex has received from the hands of the Creator, ought not to have recourse to artifice, except in the case of infirmity.' The young man who is a true republican will have nothing to do with a woman who seeks to charm by the use of adventitious aids. 'Away with you,' he will say, 'your perfumes make me feel sick. The rich materials with which you clothe yourself cost more than my harvest is worth. These habits of yours deprive me of any inclination to marry you'—and much more to the same effect.[1]

A more practical suggestion was put forward by Alexandre Deleyre, who had been a friend of Rousseau. His plan,[2] which was laid before the Convention on 28 January 1794, provided for girls' schools giving a complete training in domestic science. 'Instead of giving lessons in mathematics, geography and science, let us provide them with instruction in all suitable branches of needlework—embroidery, tapestry-work, sewing and drapery; let us even have special rooms for cooking, making pastry and confectionery, so that girls may not be ignorant of anything concerned with the business and duties of housekeeping. Let the kitchen and pantry be available to them so that they may learn all the secrets of household management, the art of preparing meals and of making preserves and confectionery.' These domestic science schools should be established in former convents in the country where there will be facilities for dairying and laundry work. It seems a pity that Deleyre's sensible suggestions were not followed up.

[1] See Hippeau, *L'Instruction publique*, I, 398–407.
[2] See *ibid*. II, 55–6.

7 The Convention. The reports of
Lanthenas and Romme

It was on the very day when Condorcet first presented his report to the Legislative Assembly that the war against Austria was declared. Contemporary difficulties and disorders inevitably distracted the minds of members from any scheme of national education, however carefully thought out and effectively presented. Thus the actual achievement of the Legislative Assembly's Committee of Public Instruction was meagre, and the importance of Condorcet's project lay rather in its long-range influence than in its immediate effects. All the same, the Assembly did, by a law of 6 June 1792, vote a sum of 100,000 francs 'for the assistance of teachers in colleges and universities who have lost their incomes through the suspension of *dîmes* and *octrois*'; but this was a mere drop in the bucket and how far it was actually paid seems doubtful. In any case it was too late to save the educational system of the country. Not only this, but on 18 August 1792 the Legislative Assembly dealt it a more serious blow than any that it had received hitherto. A law of that date followed up the previous decree of 22 March 1791 by enacting that all existing ecclesiastical orders and congregations, whether religious or lay, should be utterly abolished on the grounds that 'a State which is truly free ought not to allow any close corporation in its midst—not even those which are devoted to public instruction and have deserved well of the country.'[1]

---

[1] Refer to A. Aulard, *La Révolution française et les congrégations* (Paris, 1882), p. 41.

Members of such bodies who had been engaged in educational work were invited to continue to serve in an individual and private capacity until such time as a definite educational system could be organised. Endowments were confiscated and real property, except buildings and gardens belonging to colleges already in existence in 1789, was sold. This was the climax of a series of decrees, directed primarily against the Church, which gave the *coup de grâce* to the educational institutions which the Revolution had inherited from the *Ancien Régime*. The universities and colleges had suffered chiefly as a result of the Civil Constitution of the Clergy and its extension to teachers, because most of their personnel refused to take a step which had been anathematised by the Pope and which utterly destroyed ecclesiastical control of education. At the University of Paris, for example, out of 161 professors only 41 were prepared to take the oath. But now it was the turn of the 'little schools' and of institutions of primary education. The Christian Brothers, for example, were broken up and sought refuge in Belgium, Italy and elsewhere. The 'little schools' were affected by the August 1792 law because, even if they were staffed by lay teachers, these were still under ecclesiastical control because they had to hold the bishop's licence; and in very many cases they also were unwilling to take the civil oath. Even if they had taken it, it was a small consolation to be invited to teach as individuals when their means of livelihood had been taken from them and the State had not as yet set up any national system in which they could find a place. Yet on the whole primary education was not quite so mortally hit as was that provided by the colleges and the universities. If lay teachers in elementary schools were prepared to take the oath they were usually retained by their local authorities and allowed to continue not only to teach children, but even also to assist the *curé* in his ecclesiastical duties—that is, of course, if he also were 'assermenté', or, to use a current expression, 'intrus'—an intruder. To sum up then, by the end of 1792 the colleges and universities had to a large extent been destroyed by the abolition of *dîmes* and *octrois*, and by the exaction of the civil oath, while the primary schools had been severely affected by the law of 18 August 1792. Complaints came in from every side. For example, in October 1792 Machecoul in the department of Loire-Inférieure, laments that it has had no educational system whatever for the past three years. In November the neighbouring town of Savenay says 'The evil has now reached its height. The colleges are deserted. For the past four years our young people have been languishing in idleness'. Thus the Legislative Assembly, in spite of Condorcet and its Committee of Public Instruction, had done nothing to solve the problem of national education, but on the contrary had helped to augment it.

It remains true that, notwithstanding its immediate ineffectiveness, the project of Condorcet is a document of great interest. It was a well-conceived and thorough scheme, and under more favourable conditions it might have done something to fill the enormous void in national education. It is difficult to understand why Albert Duruy, son of the famous historian, applies to it the term 'pleine chimère'.[1] To the modern reader perhaps its most interesting and significant feature is

[1] For criticisms of Condorcet's scheme see Fortescue Tracts (London, 1899), F. R. 233 and R. 366; and also Masuyer, *Discours sur l'éducation publique* (Paris, 1795).

the place which it gives to science in the curriculum. In the latter part of the eighteenth century there had been an increasing interest in scientific subjects. Although the Oratorian, and even some of the Jesuit, *collèges* gave attention to mathematics and mechanics, the study of the natural sciences and their application to the arts and to industry owed little to the colleges and the universities. The interest was maintained and spread rather through the academies and by courses of popular lectures which were attended by women as well as by men. But, as Mme de Genlis said, speaking of the period immediately before the Revolution, 'All of a sudden the sciences became fashionable. During the winter courses in chemistry, physics and natural history were held. One never learnt anything, but one remembered a few scientific terms'.[1] Yet this was the period of Lavoisier's discoveries in chemistry and of Laplace's mathematical and astronomical researches. Condorcet himself, as an exponent of mathematics and science, wishes to make these subjects the basis of the ordinary secondary school course, and to dislodge the purely literary curriculum which had become traditional in the colleges. He is not, like Herbert Spencer, so much concerned with what knowledge is of most *use*, though he does fully realise the importance of applied science; but as far as schools are concerned he stresses chiefly the value of a scientific training in the development of the reasoning faculties. He shares with some of his educational contemporaries the rather pathetic belief that if this were secured mankind would infallibly and invariably make use of reason as a constant

[1] *Dictionnaire des étiquettes* (2 vols, Paris, 1818), I, 22. The Marquise de Châtelet (Voltaire's divine Émilie) was also an enthusiast for the sciences and even wrote some treatises on physics.

guide in life. Condorcet also sees in the application of the sciences the key to human progress and 'perfectibility'—a word which tends to recur in the educational literature of the period. But etymologically the word 'progress' simply means 'taking steps forward'; and that process the really important factor is one's in destination—a fact which even today does not always seem to be realised. Within a year and a half of the presentation of Condorcet's project a prostitute was enthroned on the high altar of Notre Dame as the 'Goddess of Reason'; and within two years Lavoisier himself did not escape the guillotine because 'La République n'a pas besoin de savants'.

The attack on the Tuileries in August 1792 and the imprisonment of the King and his family marked the downfall of royalty in France. As the Legislative Assembly was still bound by a constitution which provided for the existence of a monarch, it became necessary to establish a purely democratic government which would embody the absolute power of the sovereign people. Thus a new assembly, called the National Convention, was elected—not without disorder and intimidation and indifference. As in the case of its predecessors, the majority of the members came from the middle class, with lawyers predominating. It held its first meeting on 21 September 1792. The three years of its life coincided with one of the most stormy periods of the Revolution; it was marked by the struggles between Jacobins and Girondins, the trial and execution of the King, civil strife and external war, the massacre of political prisoners and the Reign of Terror. After the downfall of Robespierre and his execution on 28 July 1794 (10 Thermidor) affairs in France to some extent quietened down.

It was amid this welter of bloodshed and civil confusion that the educational activities of the Convention—especially during the first two years of its existence—were carried on. Amongst the various committees which it appointed was one concerned with public instruction, and this included several members who had already held a similar position under the Legislative Assembly. Condorcet was among those chosen, but he refused to serve. This committee was largely responsible for the introduction of the decimal system, the reform of the calendar, and the drawing up of further projects for a system of public instruction. Reports and proposals succeeded one another in profusion, and Albert Duruy goes so far as to say of the Convention that 'from its first to its last day it never ceased to pursue with unflagging perseverance the task of organisation which it had undertaken. Nothing could deter it from this—not external war nor civil strife nor even the Terror; and in the midst of these dreadful events it persisted in giving this matter (i.e. education) some part of its attention and care.'[1] J. Guillaume also, in a most detailed and enlightening article[2] on the educational work of the Convention, quotes the scientist and educationist Chaptal who in 1800, under the régime of the Consulate, said 'In a word, we venture to say without any reservation that it is the Convention which laid the foundation of instruction as it exists today'. He was thinking particularly, perhaps, of the Institut National which had already been adumbrated by Condorcet in his National Society of Science and Arts; but to start with the Convention very sensibly turned its attention to primary education.

[1] *L'Instruction publique de la Révolution* (Paris, 1882), p. 88.
[2] See Buisson, *Dictionnaire de pédagogie*, I, 520–71.

At the session held on 18 December 1792 François Lanthenas, who was a doctor and a member of the Committee of Public Instruction, presented in its name a report[1] on primary schools. It was realised that other stages would also have to be dealt with, but that it was necessary to make a start with elementary instruction. The content of this report was based on the plan which Condorcet had already laid before the Legislative Assembly. One or more primary schools are to be provided in each area according to the number of its inhabitants. Lanthenas stresses the dignity and importance of the primary school teacher and his work. 'If there is one function the usefulness of which renders it sacred in the eyes of the friends of liberty, it is that of the teacher in the primary school, who has been called by the confidence of the people to open up the earliest ways to knowledge and happiness and, to create in some measure, a new life for the rising generation, which is the glorious hope of the Republic.'[2] A short list of applicants for teaching posts is to be drawn up by a local committee consisting of 'hommes instruits', and the final selection is to be made by 'pères de famille et veuves'—a practice which, as has been said, was customary under the *Ancien Régime*. Teachers, who will be known as *instituteurs*,[3] are to be assured of an adequate salary determined according to the size of the population in the school area. Where possible and for accommodating the school itself, former church property and the premises of 'little schools' can be utilised.

[1] Reprinted in Guillaume, *Procès-verbaux du Comité d'Instruction Publique de la Convention Nationale* (6 vols, Paris, 1891–1907), I, 172 ff.

[2] Hippeau, *L'Instruction publique*, II, 19.

[3] This term, and also *primaire* and *secondaire*, as applied to education, date from the period of the Revolution.

Lanthenas also anticipates in some measure the monitorial system. He lays it down that 'schoolmasters and schoolmistresses too will avail themselves of the help of those pupils who are intellectually most advanced. In this way they will be able quite easily to give to four classes at the same time all the attention that is necessary to ensure their progress. Moreover, by the efforts which the most able pupils make in order to teach their comrades what they know, they will instruct themselves more effectively than by the lessons given by their master.'

The primary course will, as usual, comprise the three 'R's', together with drawing and practical work, natural history, and ethical teaching; but religious instruction is definitely debarred and no member of any religious organisation is allowed to act as *instituteur*. 'The fundamental principle of public instruction is to teach nothing but the truth. That is the reason for excluding priests.' (This statement was greeted with applause from the Assembly.) The teaching of morals, however, includes not only the principles, rights and obligations embodied in the constitution, but also lessons on patriotism, duties to parents, and kindness to animals. The primary school will take children of both sexes from the age of six, and the course will normally last four years. All teaching will be in French, and this provision is particularly important in parts of the country where French is not the vernacular language; the only exception will be areas where German is spoken, and there the teaching can be given in either language. On leaving the primary school the pupil will either go on to a higher grade of instruction or, if he takes a job, he can continue his education by part-time attendance at 'lectures publiques' which are to be given once a week by the *instituteur*. Even adults whose education has been neglected can benefit from this arrangement, which is also a reminiscence of Condorcet's project. To help in these educational activities text-books for learners and treatises on method for teachers will be prepared, and every school will have its own library.

The report of Lanthenas was embodied in a 'projet de décret sur les écoles primaires' which filled in the details. For example, the cost of providing and maintaining the schools would fall on the communes. The rules governing the appointment and remuneration of teachers were definitely laid down and it was decided that they should not be allowed to augment their incomes by undertaking church duties. The projected law and the report provoked considerable discussion and criticism. It was suggested, for example, that not only was a system of primary schools needed, but also that attendance at them should be made obligatory. The curriculum was too ambitious or it did not give enough emphasis to the teaching of republicanism. In the interest of equality the salaries of primary-school teachers should be on the same level as those of professors in schools of a higher grade. The relief of poverty was of more importance than the provision of an educational system. In the midst of arguments such as these the debate was interrupted by Marat who said that the Convention had much more urgent and serious matters to consider. He compared those who were preoccupied with educational legislation to a general who busies himself with planting trees so that they may bear fruit for the future nourishment of his soldiers who are already dying of starvation.[1] This was,

---

[1] See *Moniteur*, 12 December 1792.

in fact, the period of the King's trial and execution, soon to be followed by a declaration of war against England, Holland and Spain. An attempt was therefore made to shelve the business of public education. No action was taken on the projected law, but it was decided that the report and the speeches to which it had given rise should be printed.

In spite of this it was only two days later—on 20 December 1792—that yet another report[1] was presented to the Convention on behalf of the Committee of Public Instruction. This time it was the work of the mathematician Gilbert Romme who had had some experience as a private tutor in Russia, but who returned to France and became deputy for the department of Puy de Dôme; and, as with Condorcet's report, it outlines a complete system of national education. Romme looks back first to consider what public instruction was like in France before 1789. The universities and colleges were 'preserves of routine, error and prejudice'. The 'little schools' were insufficient in number, especially in the rural areas; their teachers were looked down upon, teaching methods were mechanical and text-books unsuitable. Of the institutions of higher education belonging to the *Ancien Régime* only the Collège de France is worth preserving. Its organisation, its comprehensiveness, and the importance and value of its teaching have set it at the summit of all public educational institutions. It should therefore either be retained or else refounded as part of a general system of public instruction.

Romme distinguishes two main stages of education: (i) what is necessary for all citizens alike; (ii) higher and professional education for the few who are qualified to

[1] Reprinted in Guillaume, *Convention*, II, 526–40.

undertake it. Both alike are necessary to the State; 'l'instruction publique n'est ni une dette ni un bienfait; c'est un besoin'. In the first group are the primary and secondary (i.e. higher primary) schools for children of both sexes, and in the second group institutes and *lycées* which will be reserved for boys only. At the head of the whole system there will be a co-ordinating and directing authority, on the lines of Condorcet's National Society of Science and Arts. Romme goes on to consider whether the State should concern itself with all these stages of instruction. He naturally believes that it should do so, and he also says that the educational system should be established and maintained at State expense. 'By absolute gratuity instruction will be more widely disseminated, more equal, more free, more independent of opinion. The arts and the sciences will be better cultivated and the country better served.' But although educational expenditure and administration should be publicly supervised, educational institutions should be free to develop their teaching and research without control. Some sort of 'academic freedom' should be retained.

The project for a decree incorporating Romme's report summarised it in eight articles. They included the points to which reference has been made. The primary schools were to give a general elementary education, the secondary schools would help the future citizen to fulfil his duties to society and to undertake ordinary technical jobs, the institutes would teach the elements of the sciences, arts and belles lettres, while the *lycées* would deal with advanced branches of knowledge. It is all rather reminiscent of previous schemes which had been discussed and shelved. But here again the Convention was too much concerned with the trial of the King; and as a matter of fact Romme's project was never even debated. None the less, the Committee of Public Instruction itself did not cease to discuss educational problems. For example, the deputy L. F. A. Arbogast raised once more the question of providing specially-composed text-books which he regarded as the best means of ensuring good teaching methods.[1] These books should be designed for all three stages of instruction, in primary and secondary schools and in institutes. Scholars and scientists will be recruited to write these works and by doing this will have deserved well of the Republic. The authors will be selected by open competition and even foreigners, as well as French citizens, will be eligible to take part. This proposal was postponed for the time being, but it was taken up again and approved at a session of the Convention on 13 June 1793.

The nationalisation of Church property and the conversion of ecclesiastics into civil servants, which had been the work of the Constituent Assembly, had had serious repercussions on educational institutions of all kinds; but on 8 March 1793 the Convention took yet another step in the same direction. On the proposal of the deputy Fouché, of Nantes, it was decided that the endowments of colleges and other establishments of public instruction, 'under whatever title they exist', should be confiscated; but the actual buildings of colleges and the living quarters of teachers and pupils were to be spared. Moreover, local authorities were required to keep such buildings in repair; and the payment of professors and *instituteurs* was to be definitely a national charge. In towns of under 3000

[1] See above pp. 30, 38, 85 and 105 ; and Arbogast's speech is reprinted in Hippeau, *L'Instruction publique*, II, 47–50.

inhabitants they were to receive 1000 to 1500 livres annually, and in larger towns 1500 to 2000 livres. It was also decided subsequently that out of the funds which had become available through the confiscation of endowments pensions should be secured to teachers and bursaries made available for pupils, preference being given to the children of citizens who had taken up arms in defence of the country. A month later (6 April) the machinery of government passed into the hands of a Committee of Public Safety which acquired almost dictatorial powers. That the importance of national education was still being realised, in spite of the abortive projects which had so often been put forward, is shown by the fact that on 30 May 1793 it was this Committee, and not the Committee of Public Instruction, which laid before the Convention a scheme for primary education; and this was adopted without discussion. It was sponsored by Bertrand Barère de Vieuzac, who was a leading member of the Committee of Public Safety and who, being something of a 'trimmer', occupied a central position between the Girondin and Jacobin extremes. This decree was on the lines which had been followed on so many previous occasions. There was to be a primary school in every area with between 400 and 1500 inhabitants, and other arrangements would be made for more densely populated areas. Each school would have one teacher who would impart the usual elementary curriculum, 'and everything which will encourage republican morality, love of country and a taste for work'. The teacher's annual salary of 1200 livres would be paid by the State; and any Frenchman holding a 'certificat de civisme' would be eligible, though *ci-devant* nobles, ecclesiastics and members of teaching congregations, whether of men or women, were to be excluded. Instruction would be free and obligatory, and parents would be constrained to send their children to school at the age of six to eight and keep them there for at least three years.

On the day after this decree had been voted the people of Paris, led by national guards, made an armed insurrection against the Convention, demanding that the Girondins should be expelled and that their leaders should be sent for trial before a Revolutionary tribunal. Among them were four members of the Committee of Public Instruction, including Lanthenas who had been responsible for the report of December 1792. He was, however, set free owing to the intervention of Marat. From this time onwards the Girondins as a political party ceased to exist, and as they had been a predominant group in the Committee of Public Instruction it might have been expected that the Convention would now lose its interest in educational matters. But on 3 June it decided to re-appoint its committees—including, of course, that concerned with public instruction; and it was not long before this re-entered upon the scene with yet another project dealing mainly with elementary education and including many of the proposals which had characterised earlier schemes.

8 The Sieyès–Daunou–Lakanal report. National festivals. Lepelletier's project

The downfall of the Girondins left the power in the hands of the Jacobin extremists—the party known as the 'Mountain'. One of its first acts was to draw up a revised republican constitution, and this was accepted by the Convention on 24 June 1793. However, like so many Assembly decrees it was never put into effect and was formally suspended in the following October. Dictatorial power was exercised by a new Committee of Public Safety (known as the Great Committee of Public Safety), of which Robespierre was the most conspicuous member. This initiated the Reign of Terror, but it also succeeded in crushing civil revolt at home and repelling the threat of foreign invasion. The constitution of 1793 did however contain a reference to education. 'Society', it said, 'ought to foster with all its power the development of reason among the people (*raison publique*) and put instruction within the reach of all citizens.'[1] It was on 26 June 1793 also—only two days after the acceptance of the new constitution—that there appeared yet another educational plan relating mainly to elementary education. This time it was the joint work of three members of the Committee of Public Instruction. There was first of all Emmanuel Sieyès, who had formerly been a priest but who had been elected to the National Assembly as representative of the *Tiers État* and had soon afterwards renounced his orders.[2] He

[1] See J. M. Thompson, *French Revolution Documents* (Oxford, 1933), p. 241 and F. Boursin and A. Challamel, *Dictionnaire de la Révolution française* (Paris, 1893), p. 916. [2] See above, p. 57.

developed into a convinced republican and voted for the execution of the King; but he was no extremist and in fact had belonged to the central party between the Jacobins and the Girondins. It was this party which was most strongly represented in the Committee of Public Instruction. The second member of the triumvirate was Jean-Claude-François Daunou who had been an Oratorian and had therefore had considerable experience as a teacher. This order on the whole was not unfavourable to the Revolution in its early days, and for this reason it had been less severely persecuted than some of the other teaching congregations. Daunou had even presented to the Constituent Assembly in 1790 a plan of education 'in the name of the public teachers of the Oratory'; but this document was never discussed by it. Daunou accepted the Civil Constitution of the Clergy and, on being elected to the Convention in 1791, he also renounced his orders. Like Sieyès, although a staunch republican he remained a member of the central party. The educational project of 1793 was mainly the work of Sieyès and Daunou, but it was presented to the Assembly by a third member of the Committee of Public Instruction, Joseph Lakanal. He also had been a member of a teaching order—that of the Doctrinaires—and had taught in several of their colleges. He was one of the representatives sent to the Convention by the department of Ariège, but it was not until March 1793 that he was admitted as a member of the Committee of Public Instruction. Like his two colleagues, he was not an extremist. Even before his appearance as 'reporter' for their co-operative educational scheme, Lakanal had already presented several projects dealing mainly with matters of higher education, and he also revived the proposals of Arbogast with reference to the composition of text-books.[1] But it is the 'Project for a National System of Education' which we have now to consider.

The object of the schools which it described was 'to give children of both sexes the instruction which is necessary for French citizens'. There would be one school to every thousand inhabitants in all parts of the Republic, and extra schools in more densely populated areas. The first lessons in reading and writing would be given to both sexes together by a mistress; but after that schools for boys and girls would be separate and they would be taught by a teacher of the appropriate sex. In each district there would be a 'bureau d'inspection' which would supervise the business of the local schools and examine and select the teachers, but their actual appointment would have to be confirmed by the administrative council of the district. There would be standard rates of salary for teachers in all parts of the country alike, but the scales would be reviewed every ten years. When on duty and on state occasions the teacher would wear a medal inscribed 'Celui qui instruit est un second père'. In addition to the local education authority there is to be a Commission Centrale de l'Instruction Publique, consisting of twelve members, and this will co-ordinate and standardise the general organisation of the national educational system.

The education given in the State schools will deal with the 'whole man'—'elle embrasse tout l'homme'; and for this reason it will be intellectual, physical and moral. After a preliminary course in reading and writing, the pupils will proceed to learn arithmetic and the elements of geometry, physics, geography, and their duties as citizens. They are also to have practice

[1] See above, p. 108.

in the use of dictionaries. Physical exercises will be included in order to promote health and agility, and even singing and dancing are prescribed. Arrangements are to be made for periodic medical inspection by the 'officier de santé du district'. Pupils are to be taken on visits to hospitals and prisons, and encouraged to help their parents in agricultural and domestic work; and in school-time the boys are to have periods of military drill while the girls are busy with needlework. Children who have worked well and shown themselves models of good conduct and general helpfulness are to be rewarded with prizes; and these will be distributed on special occasions when the public will be invited to attend. There is no mention in Lakanal's report of either gratuity or obligation, but it would seem that these are implied so far as elementary education at any rate is concerned. The final sections of the project, however, lay it down that 'the law has no power to infringe the right which citizens have of opening private and independent schools or courses at any stage of instruction, and of carrying these on in any way they think fit'. All the same, such educational institutions, including boarding-schools, are to be under the supervision of the district *bureaux d'inspection* and the Central Commission for Public Instruction. The scheme therefore seems to suggest that primary education is to be the sole responsibility of the State, but that higher education is to be left to private initiative. It is, however, clearly stated that provision is to be made for grants to children who need assistance in order to study 'connaissances supérieures' in independent schools run by private teachers. These grants will be recommended by the *bureaux* and confirmed by the commission.

Lakanal's report, then, says little about education

beyond the primary level, but it does instruct the
Central Commission to see to the provision of libraries,
museums and botanical gardens, and to encourage
academies and other institutions designed to further
progress in the arts and their applications, 'such as
lycées and institutes'. But a more interesting section is
that which deals with national festivals. The importance
of these for fostering republican enthusiasm and, for
that reason, using them as a means of propaganda in the
national schools had been realised from the early days of
the Revolution. The solemn celebration of special days
is peculiar to no particular age or country—witness
our own Day of Remembrance at the Cenotaph or the
Independence Day celebrations in the United States.
But life under the *Ancien Régime* had always been
diversified by processions and other ritual activities
associated with special saints' days or feasts of the
Church. It was no doubt that to supply the lack of these
functions, to which the people had become accustomed,
the Revolution inaugurated a new calendar of national
festivals; and it was not unnatural that in view of their
propaganda value, children and schools should have
been encouraged to take an active part in such
commemorations. From medieval times the pupils in
the 'little schools' had had their own special celebrations on the festivals of St Nicholas and St Catherine,
who were the particular patrons of boys and girls; and
the ceremonies connected with the boy-bishop on
Innocents' Day were as well-known in France as they
once were in this country. Even the University of
Paris had its celebrations on the festival of St Denis
when the *Lendi*[1] was observed, or on that of St Charle-

[1] See H. C. Barnard, *The French Tradition in Education*, pp. 12–13,
14, 16, 187.

magne who had been adopted as the patron of the University. With this tradition so firmly rooted in the lives of the French people and so closely linked with educational establishments at every level, it is not surprising to find the importance of national festivals discussed in several of the projects which have already been described. A reference to this subject had even been made in the constitution of 1791: 'There shall be established national festivals to keep citizens in mind of the Constitution, to promote brotherhood among them, and to make them faithful to the Constitution, the country and the laws.'[1] Among the documents relating to education which were written by Mirabeau and published after his death there was a memorandum concerning the 'Organisation of National Festivals'. Their object will be to commemorate the Revolution and the Constitution. 'By means of them you will speak to the people of the events which have given birth to our new institutions.' Mirabeau therefore proposes that every year there shall be four military and four civilian festivals, as well as a grand national celebration. The emotions which they will stimulate and the manner in which these will be expressed are described in a highly rhetorical manner. Similarly in Talleyrand's educational report *fêtes nationales* are regarded as a means of instilling republican principles— 'vous voudrez conduire les hommes au bien par la route du plaisir'. Condorcet again, in his project for a system of public instruction, says 'The national festivals will remind the dwellers in the country and the citizens in the towns of the glorious days of liberty, by consecrating the memory of men whose lives have been made honourable by their virtues, and by cele-

[1] See J. M. Thompson, *French Revolution Documents*, p. 113.

brating their deeds of devotion and courage; and they will teach them to value the duties which they have learnt in this way'. But it is in the report presented to the Convention by Lakanal that the educational importance of the national festivals is particularly stressed. This section of the document was the work more especially of the ex-priest Sieyès. There will be four days of celebration common to all parts of the country, and these will commemorate the Brotherhood of the Human Race (1 January); the Revolution (14 July); the Abolition of Royalty and Establishment of the Republic (10 August); and the French People, on the day when the revised constitution was accepted. There were also to be festivals of special significance to young people—e.g. those dedicated to Paternal Love, Maternal Tenderness, Filial Piety, Infancy and Youth. In addition, each canton, district and department would have its own special festival days. 'The pupils of the national schools will take part in the national fêtes, and will have a special place assigned to them... They will, in particular, be practised in singing and dancing in order to be able to take part in the national fêtes.'[1] However, there seems to have been a tendency for the enthusiasm to wear off and the whole movement did not escape criticism. A pamphlet dating from about 1794 refers to what it calls *festomanie*; and in another published probably about the same time the scientist Jean-Henri Hassenfratz warned his hearers that while France was organising her festivals other nations were organising their industries, and they might well destroy

[1] There is a good short account of these fêtes in A. Babeau, *L'École de village pendant la Révolution* (Paris, 1881), chap. ii, and also in Duruy, *L'Instruction publique de la Révolution* (Paris, 1882), chap. vi. For a more detailed treatment see J. Tiersot, *Les fêtes et les chants de la Révolution française* (Paris, 1908).

her manufactures and commerce. It was not by means of festivals that England and the United States were attaining economic and political power.[1]

During the discussion which followed the presentation of Lakanal's report there was a good deal of criticism. Hassenfratz, who was a convinced Jacobin—in fact a Montagnard—condemned the scheme because it was largely the work of an ex-priest, Sieyès, and in particular he deprecated the creation of a Central Commission of Public Instruction. 'This', he said, 'is a new over-ruling aristocracy which Sieyès wants to set up on the lines of the Sorbonne, so as to direct public opinion according to his will.' The Jacobins, who were now in control of the Convention, applauded this point of view, and the Sieyès–Daunou–Lakanal project was set aside. But the discussion dragged on and both Sieyès and Daunou wrote replies to the criticisms which had been made, and these documents were published. Their attempts produced no effect; but Lakanal returned to the charge later on under more favourable conditions—as we shall see in due course.

Meanwhile the Mountain proceeded to consider a scheme which went far beyond anything which had hitherto been proposed and which reflects, perhaps, the violent extremes of the stage which the Revolution had by this time reached. It was the work of Louis-Michel Lepelletier, Marquis de Saint-Fargeau.[2] He had been elected to the States-General as a representative of the

[1] J. H. Hassenfratz, *Réflexions sommaires sur l'éducation publique* (n.d.), pp. 6–7. See also Guillaume, *Procès-verbaux du Comité d'Instruction Publique de la Convention Nationale*, II, 426.

[2] See Guillaume, *Convention*, II, 35–54, and A. Sicard, *L'Éducation morale et civique avant et pendant la Révolution* (Paris, 1884), pp. 496–501. The name is sometimes spelt 'Lepeletier' or 'Le Peletier'; but the spelling 'Lepelletier' is that given in the *Biographie universelle* (vol. XXIV, Paris, 1819).

nobility, but had supported the abolition of his order in June 1790. He was elected to the Convention by the Department of Yonne, and voted for the execution of the King. On 20 January 1793, the day after this had been decreed, a fanatic royalist assassinated Lepelletier, who thus became, as it were, a martyr and hero in the cause of the Revolution. It was this fact that gave a special prestige and interest to a plan for a national system of education which was found among his papers after his death. Robespierre had been appointed one of six commissioners who were to deal with educational matters; and Lepelletier's document[1] was read to the Convention by him on 13 July 1793—the very day on which Marat was assassinated by Charlotte Corday who regarded him as responsible for the proscription of the Girondins.

Robespierre began by saying that his audience would be listening to Lepelletier discussing national education and in so doing would realise the greatness of the loss which they had suffered at his death. He went on to declare that his own ideas on the subject would have included a much wider scheme than that suggested by Lepelletier. 'Considering the depths to which the human race has been degraded by the vices of our former social system, I am convinced of the need to effect a complete regeneration, and, if I may so express it, to create a new people.' However, Lepelletiers' scheme would provide a system of education applying to all children alike, whatever the family circumstances might be. Thus attendance at the elementary school would be obligatory, as soon as this could be made effective, and the expense would be met from public funds. In order to effect this in every canton there will

[1] Reprinted in Guillaume, *Convention*, II, 35–54, and in Hippeau, *L'Instruction publique*, I, 342–86.

be levied a graduated education rate which will fall most heavily on the more wealthy citizens. Not only this, but Lepelletier, borrowing the theories of Plato and the practice of Sparta, regards children as belonging not to their parents, but to the nation. He would therefore take them from their families at the age of five and instal them in State boarding-schools, where they will undergo a strict régime 'sous la sainte loi de l'égalité'. They will all receive the same plain but wholesome food —no meat or wine—and even wear the same kind of clothes. Boys will remain at school till the age of twelve and girls till eleven. Children will learn to read, write and cipher, and the boys will be given some notions of measuring and surveying. They will also learn by heart national songs and the most important events in the history of free peoples and of the Revolution. They will be given some information as to the constitution of their country, the fundamental principles of morality and the elements of rural and domestic economy; but there is to be no religious instruction. A large part of the course for both sexes will consist of practical work. The boys will be employed on the roads or in neighbouring factories or even do manual jobs in the school itself. The girls will learn needlework and laundry work and can also help in factories. It is to be hoped that (as in 'schools of industry') the profits earned by the labour of pupils may be devoted to the expenses of running their school, but the main cost of the scheme will be met by the cantonal levy. The schools themselves, which will be called 'maisons d'égalité',[1] will be founded wherever they are needed and can be housed in buildings belonging to the nation—e.g.

---

[1] This name was suggested not by Lepelletier himself, but by another *montagnard* extremist, François Bourdon.

ci-devant religious houses or places where émigrés used to live. One master to every fifty pupils will be sufficient and he will have a fixed salary of 400 livres together with an allowance of board equal to twice that of the eldest children. The administration of the school will be in the hands of fifty-two heads of families, and each of them will undertake one week's supervision duty during the course of the year. In addition to this there will be a full 'governors' meeting' every month. The housework of the schools will be undertaken by the children themselves and no servants are to be employed.

In Lepelletier's scheme, then, the school is made an instrument for conditioning citizens according to a prescribed pattern. No concessions are to be made to differences of ability or physique or disposition. 'To develop in children a good habit of life; to increase their powers; to encourage their growth; to foster in them strength, dexterity and activity; to render them insensitive to fatigue, the rigours of the weather and temporary deprivation of the necessities of life'—this is the aim of the truly Spartan régime which is prescribed, and all alike must submit to it. Moreover Lepelletier goes on to say 'The whole being of the child belongs to us...Everything which belongs to the Republic should be cast in a republican mould'. If any parent objects to abandoning his children to the care of the State he is to be punished by being deprived of his civic rights and condemned to pay a double education rate.

Although Lepelletier begins his report by criticising Condorcet's scheme, he accepts its four stages of instruction—primary and secondary schools, institutes and *lycées*; but he devotes most of what he has to say to the first of these stages which has just been described. When, however, children have spent their preliminary six or seven years under the care of the State boarding-school 'it will be time to hand them over to some form of manual work'. Agriculture and industry will offer careers for the majority of school-leavers; but a small proportion will continue their education in the higher schools, and these also will provide gratuitous instruction. The course in the secondary school will last four years, in the institutes five, and in the *lycées* four. At the end of each stage a selection of about half the pupils will be made, and these will be admitted to the next one. Lepelletier gives no details as to proposed courses or curricula in establishments of higher education.

In the debate which followed the reading of Lepelletier's project this not unnaturally came in for a good deal of criticism. For example, the Abbé Grégoire,[1] who had been a representative of the clergy in the States-General and one of the first ecclesiastics to take the civil oath, while proclaiming his belief in com-pulsory education for all children alike, took exception to the 'maisons d'égalité'. The whole scheme would be too costly and it would hardly be possible to deprive parents of their children's labour in agricultural work at certain seasons of the year. In any case, family life is beneficial for children and parents alike. 'Nothing can replace the kindness of a father, the caresses of a mother. Let us leave children the opportunity of practising every-day filial piety.' Grégoire therefore rejected Lepelletier's scheme on the ground of its expense, the difficulty of putting it into practice, and its ethical

[1] A. Gazier, *Études sur l'histoire religieuse de la Révolution française* (Paris, 1887), is a detailed account of Grégoire's activities during the Revolution.

implications. A similar point of view was expressed by the scientist Antoine-François, Comte de Fourcroy, who had been supervising methods of providing gunpowder for the use of the republican armies and had recently been elected a Paris deputy in the place of Marat. But Robespierre had no reservations as to the project. 'I hesitate no longer', he said. 'It ought to be adopted.'

In the end, on 13 August 1793, Lepelletier's scheme for 'maisons d'égalité', with certain modifications, was accepted. But an important amendment, due largely to Danton, was made. 'Let us have', he said, 'a common education for all alike. Everything grows narrow under a domestic education; everything expands under public education. I too am a father; but my son does not belong to me. He belongs to the Republic.[1] It is for her to decide what he ought to do in order to serve her well.' But he realises the force of the argument that in rural areas parents will need the assistance of children in agricultural work. 'Very well, let there be national establishments in which children will be gratuitously instructed, boarded and lodged, but also classes to which citizens who wish to keep their children at home can send them.' The Convention thereupon passed a decree to this effect; but as usual it was a dead letter. On the following 20 October it was rescinded without opposition on the motion of Léonard Bourdon,[2] who was one of the Commission of Six and had had practical experience as founder and director of an orphanage which he called 'La Société des Jeunes Français'.

[1] M.-E. Petit went so far as to say that the child belonged to society from the moment of its conception (see *Moniteur*, 22 January 1792).
[2] He was apparently no relation of François Bourdon (see above, p. 120).

123

9 Romme's report of 1793. The cult of the Supreme Being

While the debates on Lepelletier's plan were in progress the Convention was entering upon the most critical period of its history. In order to make headway against foreign invasion and civil rebellion in the Vendée and the South, the *levée en masse* was enforced by a decree of 10 August 1793. 'All French people, whatever their age or sex, are called by their country to defend liberty.' In the event this meant a general conscription for men between eighteen and twenty-five; but there were also frantic efforts to provide the armies with food and ammunition; and the law of the Maximum controlled the prices of articles of food. Revolutionary tribunals, set up not only in Paris but all over France, dealt with political offences and arrested and condemned to death those whom they suspected of being likely to oppose the existing régime. Between August 1793 and July 1794 the number of those sent to the guillotine increased steadily week by week. This is indeed the Reign of Terror; yet even amid these horrors the Convention still managed to turn its attention from time to time to educational matters.

On 15 September 1793 it received a deputation from the department of Paris, together with representatives of several popular societies in the area. They presented a petition on the subject of national education. They criticised the system of higher instruction bequeathed to the Republic by the *Ancien Régime*, on the grounds that it was 'éminemment défectueuse' and accessible only to the favoured few. Thus there is need for schools where young republicans will learn whatever is needed in the service of the community, and it is the duty of the nation to provide them. The Convention has discussed educational projects and voted educational systems, yet practically nothing has been achieved. In addition to a plan for primary education there is an urgent need for a system of higher instruction. The academic year is just beginning and yet such colleges as remain in Paris and elsewhere are still 'dedicated to medieval barbarism', and not much better than training-grounds for the priesthood. They ought to be reformed and made accessible to even the poorest citizens. The petition therefore demanded the establishment of secondary schools with a two-year course giving instruction in mathematics and science and their applications, as well as other subjects which are not specified. These schools would lead on first to institutes and then to *lycées*. In the latter the courses would be organised in four sections. The first would comprise mathematics and physics; the second, languages and literature; the third, ethics and political science; the fourth, a curious hotch-potch of useful and fine arts including 'l'art de nourrir, de vêtir, d'abriter, et de se défendre', as well as painting, sculpture, music, acting and elocution.

This petition was accepted by the Convention with only one dissentient, and Lakanal, speaking on behalf of the six Commissioners, said that it was in effect a plan which they had already developed. It was decided that the scheme should be applied not only to Paris, but should also be extended to the whole of the Republic. It was to come into force on the following 1 November, and in consequence all existing Faculty of Arts colleges, as well as the faculties of theology, law and medicine throughout the Republic were to be suppressed. But on the very next day (16 September) Jacques-Michel Couppé,[1] deputy of the department of Oise, who had been the sole opponent of the scheme from the beginning, returned to the charge. He had on a previous occasion spoken against the plan which Lakanal had put forward in July 1793; and he now claimed that the proposed system of higher education, of which Lakanal was again the sponsor, would in effect create a new kind of aristocracy—that of the intelligentsia. This gave rise to a heated discussion and it was decided to suspend further action for the moment. In the event the whole matter was yet once again shelved, and the remaining establishments of higher education, such as they were, continued to exist.

The Commission of Six, to which had been entrusted the oversight of public education, had run into difficulties to which Couppé also drew attention. 'The Commission', he said, 'which you charged with the duty of presenting a plan of education has got stuck in its course. It is composed of six members. Three of them are committed to a system and will not give way, and the other three also refuse to compromise. I propose therefore that you add three more members to the Commission.' This was done, and Romme (who had been responsible for the project of 20 December 1792) was one of those chosen. The augmented body proceeded to evolve yet another 'projet de décret sur les écoles nationales'. On 20 October 1793 this was presented to the Convention on behalf of the Commission by Romme himself. It was a lengthy document,[2] but its main proposals were as follows: All colleges and

[1] The name is sometimes spelt 'Coupé'.
[2] Reprinted in Guillaume, *Procès-verbaux du Comité d'Instruction Publique de la Convention Nationale*, v, 526–40.

faculties of law and medicine, as well as all 'little schools' of any kind, are to be suppressed. This reform is to take effect as soon as new establishments can be provided. The national educational system is to be reorganised in two main sections: (i) that necessary for all citizens alike; (ii) special types of instruction to meet the various needs of society. Every child will attend a State school from the age of six, but this obligatory first section will be sub-divided into primary and secondary stages. The curriculum will be much the same in both, though it will of course be graduated according to the age and ability of the pupils. In their first years at school the children will learn to read, write and speak their native French, and they will also be given some elementary knowledge of the history of the Revolution and the geography of France. There will be lessons on the rights and duties of the citizen, together with gymnastics and military drill. Work in the fields and visits to workshops and factories will help children to realise the dignity of labour. In the second stage of the obligatory course these subjects will be taken further and there will be added to them the elements of physics and natural history with some practice in the use of instruments and apparatus. There will be schools of the first section in every commune of 400 to 1500 inhabitants, and more in proportion; and they will be co-educational. There is no indication of the age of transition from the first section of obligatory 'écoles d'enfance' to the second stage of specialised schools catering for such adolescents as are qualified to proceed to higher education. In these latter the curriculum will include foreign and classical languages with some notions of law and history and other subjects necessary for the future citizen. Science, mathematics and their application to human needs, such as food, clothing, preservation, defence, will form an important part of the course. In this connection the existing schools of mines, artillery, engineering, medicine, agriculture and oriental languages are to be retained until such time as they can be re-organised. The number of teachers assigned to any particular school will be determined not only by its size, but also by the type of curriculum which it offers. The teachers—who are to be called *instituteurs* in whatever kind of school they serve—are to be 'fonctionnaires publiques' and should be accorded an honourable status.

All this covered ground which was already familiar, but during the subsequent discussion some additional provisions were added to Romme's original project. One of them dealt with the salaries of teachers. *Instituteurs* were to receive annually 1000 to 2400 livres according to the size of the commune in which they served; *institutrices* would be paid one-fifth less. This was in excess of what had been allotted in previous schemes, but it must be remembered that owing to depreciation in the value of *assignats*[1] and the effects of civil and foreign war there had been a considerable rise in the cost of living. The Central Commission would have the duty of inspecting the academic work of the schools, but the local heads of families would appoint a 'magistrat des mœurs' who would oversee matters of discipline and moral tone.

So the debate went on, with proposals and criticisms following close on one another. The general feeling was that primary education was the really urgent problem; and on 19 December 1793 a plan was presented by Gabriel Bouquier, who was a poet and an artist; and it was accepted. According to it education is to be free and is a public responsibility. Citizens who wish to open

[1] See below, p. 180 n.

independent schools must inform the authorities of the municipality or commune of their intention and must furnish a certificate of 'civisme' and 'bonnes mœurs'. Teachers are to be under the supervision of the local authority and of parents. If they teach anything contrary to republican laws or morals they are to be punished severely. Elementary text-books for inculcating republicanism are to be supplied by the Committee of Public Instruction. Teachers' salaries will be paid by the State and will everywhere be on the same basis and calculated according to the number of pupils in the school. *Instituteurs* are not to take boarders or do outside work. Pupils in primary schools must be at least six years of age before being admitted. The age for leaving the primary school is not specified, but pupils must either go to work on the land or else learn some trade or profession which will be useful to society. If they have not done so by the age of twenty they are to be deprived of the exercise of civic rights for ten years. The question of providing suitable text-books for elementary education was raised again by Grégoire on 23 January 1794. It was decided that a competition should be organised to provide treatises on the nurture and care of children in their earliest pre-school years, as well as on teaching methods for the use of *instituteurs* and on various school subjects for the pupils themselves.[1] The works submitted were examined by the Committee of Public Instruction, and as a beginning seven were selected and these were ordered to be published at the expense of the State.[2] They included elementary text-books on grammar, arithmetic, natural history, re-

[1] See *Moniteur*, 30 January 1794.
[2] Even when such text-books as these had been compiled and published it appears that they were not used to any great extent, except perhaps in Paris itself.

publican morals (with appropriate didactic verses) and swimming—a curious curriculum.

Grégoire also emphasised, as Talleyrand had done,[1] the importance of having in all parts of France a standard language—the language of the Rights of Man—as a unifying and nationalising instrument. Federalism and superstition, he says, speak Breton; the émigrés speak German, the counter-revolutionists speak Italian; and fanaticism speaks Basque. French citizens should speak one and the same language—French; and all patois should be abolished. State schools should cooperate to ensure this. As the deputy Barère said at a séance of the Convention on 27 January 1794, 'la langue d'un peuple libre doit être une et la même pour tous'.

The chief critic of Romme's plan of October 1793 had been Antoine-Claire Thibaudeau who saw in it the establishment of a new educational government in the heart of the Republic, and who said that the formation of a State corps of teachers implied 'une nouvelle espèce de clergé'. The Revolution had destroyed the guilds of the *Ancien Régime*, and now a pedagogic hierarchy is to be set up which will consist of 'régulateurs plenipotentiaires des mœurs, des goûts, des usages'. Such people will easily make themselves arbiters of the liberties and destinies of the nation. The speaker was supported by Fourcroy. 'Laisser faire', he said, 'est ici le grand secret et la seule route de succès les plus certains...Plus de corporations, plus de privilèges dangereux pour la liberté.'[2] The extreme

[1] See above, p. 72.

[2] See the whole speech which is reprinted in Hippeau, *L'Instruction publique*, II, 107–10. The same sentiment was expressed again by Boulay de la Meurthe, a member of the Conseil des Cinq-cents under the Directory—'laissez faire, voilà la grande maxime qui doit diriger le gouvernement.' (See Hippeau, *op. cit.* II, 311.)

point of view was: why have schools at all?—and some speakers went almost to this length, at any rate so far as higher education was concerned. On 11 December 1793 the deputy Gabriel Bouquier declared that 'free nations have no need of a caste of speculative savants. Pure science separates from the rest of society the individuals who cultivate it, and in the end it proves a poison which infects, weakens and destroys a republic'.[1] One is reminded of the verdict on Lavoisier. Bouquier went on to declare that 'the real schools, the best, the most useful, the simplest, and those in which youth can receive a truly republican education, are the meetings of committees especially in republican clubs,[2] whether in departments, districts or communes. The Revolution, by establishing national festivals, by creating popular associations and clubs, has provided everywhere inexhaustible sources of instruction. Let us not therefore substitute for this organisation—simple and sublime, as the people have created it—an artificial organisation based on academic statutes which should no longer infect a regenerated nation.' A decree was thereupon adopted which permitted freedom to teach with the requirement only of a certificate of *civisme* and good morals, but without any intellectual test. All the same, this freedom was often more apparent than real. The certificate of *civisme* and *bonnes mœurs* had to be obtained from the council of the commune in which the teacher lived, and his school was to be under its supervision. If his teaching contravened republican principles he was to be punished 'according to the

[1] *Ibid.* II, 17.
[2] On the part played by clubs and popular societies in national education during the Revolution see Louis-Grimaud, *Histoire de la liberté d'enseignement en France*, II, 20–2, and A. Duruy, *L'Instruction publique de la Révolution*, pp. 149–56.

gravity of the offence'. It is obvious therefore that there was a political control over the school, even if it were nominally independent. Moreover, the teacher according to the letter of the law was required to use the text-books prescribed by the government, so that there was in this way also some check on the actual instruction. The Loi Bouquier remained in force until the end of the Reign of Terror. In some areas (e.g. the district of Strasbourg) a fair number of schools were organised under these conditions; but in many parts of France the law was not effectively applied, and parents were often unwilling to send their children to schools which were in some way associated with political clubs and similar societies.

It was in fact no easy task to force the population as a whole to accept some of the extremes which the Revolution had now reached. Reference has already been made to the national fêtes which were designed not only to stimulate enthusiasm for the republican régime, but also to take the place of the ceremonies and festivals of the Catholic Church, which for many centuries had been part of the life of the French people. But it is hard to eradicate deeply implanted religious sentiment, and in endeavouring to do so the Republic had to find something to put in its place. Even Rousseau in his *Social Contract* had a chapter on 'Civil Religion', and in it had said that it is very important for the State that every citizen 'should have a religion that may make him delight in his duties'. It was with this aim that the Feast of Reason was celebrated in Nôtre Dame on 10 November 1793, under the inspiration of Robespierre. It was followed on 8 June 1794 by the inauguration of a State religion called the Cult of the Supreme Being. During the winter of 1793–4 churches all over France

132

had been compulsorily closed for Catholic worship and, in spite of resistance in some quarters, attempts were made to spread the new religion. The code of conduct which it inculcated was 'to detest bad faith and despotism, to punish tyrants and traitors, to assist the unfortunate, to respect the weak, to defend the oppressed, to do all the good one can to one's neighbour, to behave with justice towards all men'. Every tenth day (the *décadi* of the new revolutionary calendar which had been introduced in September 1793) there would be celebrations in honour of such abstractions as nature and humanity, as well as commemorations of the chief events of the Revolution. There had already been a proposal to associate the school with religious reform along these lines. On 1 October 1793 Michel-Edmé Petit, in a project which was not actually discussed, had advocated that in all establishments of public education there should be religious instruction. But it was not to be the teaching of any particular accepted religion, but rather the vague deism which Robespierre afterwards developed into the Cult of the Supreme Being. 'The principles of natural religion', said Petit, 'are the great truths recognised by all religions since time immemorial. They are founded on belief in the existence of God who controls nature, who is the father of all men alike and the source of all justice.'[1] All the same, the teaching itself was in the event to be given a definite republican bias. Children in school were supplied with manuals which would help them to follow the worship of Reason and the Supreme Being.[2] There

[1] Hippeau, *L'Instruction publique*, II, 86.
[2] For details see Louis-Grimaud, *Histoire de la liberté d'enseignement en France*, pp. 171–6, and A. Sicard, *L'Éducation morale et civique avant et pendant la Révolution*, pp. 308–14 and 406–48.

133

was, for example, the 'Office of *Décadi*', which contained 'hymns and prayers for use in the temples of Reason'; and various republican catechisms were composed to replace those of the Church. There was even a new republican parody of the versified Ten Commandments which had been taught to children under the *Ancien Régime*. Then there was the book of 'republican epistles and gospels for all the *décadis* of the year, for the use of young *sans-culottes*'. Some idea of the contents of this work may be gained from the fact that the first epistle consists of a panegyric of Rousseau. Here too is a specimen of the gospels: 'At that time[1] a *sans-culotte* said to his brothers: Beware of fine speakers who in your assemblies seek only to develop their own opinions with a kind of pretentiousness and mystery. Verily, they are deceivers. Beware also of him who speaks for a whole hour and only expresses the same opinion. He is seeking to lead you astray. He is aiming at some important position, and once he has extorted it from you he will mock at your credulity.' In addition to studying manuals such as these in school, children were taken to meetings of the local political club on *décadis*, and there they were welcomed by the president and made to recite the Rights of Man or answer questions from the republican catechism or sing hymns in honour of liberty or the motherland. It was certainly a form of compulsory religious instruction. But once the novelty of the new cult and its celebrations began to wear off there was a decline in whatever enthusiasm had been worked up. Speaking generally, the support which the schools gave to the official cult seems to have been rather half-hearted and

[1] In the Roman liturgy the reading of the Gospel is always prefaced with the words 'In illo tempore'.

parents, particularly in rural areas, tended to resist attempts to substitute the new religion for the Catholicism to which they had been accustomed and which they wished to pass on to their children. The revolt in the Vendée had been due in some considerable measure to resentment at the anti-Church measures of the government.

10 L'École Polytechnique. L'École des Armes. L'École de Mars

Although there were some extremists who condemned selective higher education on the ground that it was non-egalitarian and unnecessary for a free people, the Republic certainly did need scientists. A nation at war and faced with enemies on all its frontiers urgently required the services of technical experts in the military applications of engineering and mining, in the art of fortification, and in the manufacture of armaments. Under the *Ancien Régime* there had been separate schools of military and civil engineering. The former— the École du Génie Militaire—had been established at Mézières in 1748 and was reserved for cadets of noble birth. In 1791 it was moved to Metz, and at the same time the theoretical part of the two-year course was transferred to the civil engineering school, the École des Ponts et Chaussées, which was situated in Paris. This latter had been founded in 1747, but it had not proved so successful as the military school. It lacked laboratories and a library, and it was also insufficiently staffed. Some of the teaching was even done by the more advanced pupils and, as might be expected, it tended to be largely rule-of-thumb instruction and not based on a sound knowledge of science; but, as there were no special conditions of entry, some of the pupils were said to have had hardly any knowledge even of arithmetic. By 1793 the situation had become serious. The only solution was to close the existing schools and start afresh; and a project was put forward in the name of the Committees of War and of Public Works for the

136

fusion of the two institutions. 'The present situation is so urgent that it is necessary to employ civil engineers for the same duties as military engineers. It is right that those who do the same work should be put in the same class and be placed on the same footing, and that they should all be equal in the eyes of the law.'

In spite of the urgency it was a little time before the scheme started moving. This was obviously due to the increasingly disturbed state of public affairs. In October 1793 an emergency government was established which confirmed the supremacy of the Great Committee of Public Safety and in which Robespierre was a leading spirit. The Reign of Terror was in full swing and Jacobin policy was for the time successful. Civil insurrection in the Vendée was suppressed and by a series of victories France was delivered from the danger of foreign invasion. But the Jacobins quarrelled among themselves and finally Robespierre was arrested on a charge of aiming at a dictatorship, and he was declared an outlaw. On the 10 Thermidor (28 July 1794) he went to the guillotine. After this, the horrors which had distracted France began to abate somewhat, and a reaction set in which swept away the Jacobin party and its organisations.

It was against this sort of background that the Convention carried on its discussions concerning the organisation of a school of military and civil engineering. On 11 March 1794 Bertrand Barère, who was a member of the Great Committee of Public Safety and had already interested himself in educational matters, proposed the formation of an institution devoted to this work. 'It is in the public interest', he said, 'that you should place in one central institution the different military, civil and hydraulic operations which are based on the same principles and necessitate the same preliminary studies.' The Convention, realising the need for such a college, decided to adopt a plan which was laid before it on 24 September 1794 by the scientist Fourcroy. He emphasised the country's need for 'engineers trained in the construction and maintenance of fortifications, the attack on camps and their defence ...the construction and maintenance of communications by land and water, roads, bridges, canals, locks, seaports, lighthouses...the production of maps, whether terrestrial or maritime, the prospecting and working of minerals, the smelting of metals and the perfecting of metallurgic processes.' But all this technical instruction was to be firmly based on a sound scientific training, and particularly upon mathematics and physics. Thus the new institution would not only train engineers of all kinds but would also 're-establish the teaching of the exact sciences which has been suspended owing to the crises of the Revolution'. Fourcroy carried the war into the enemies' camp by condemning 'the conspiracy hatched by the partisans of tyranny in order to banish the sciences from the territory of the Republic'.

The new college, which was named L'École Centrale des Travaux Publics, was opened on 10 December 1794. Its course, which lasted three years, was 'based on the general scientific principles which are equally indispensable for civil and military engineers alike'. A staff of the most eminent scientists of the day was appointed. It included Fourcroy himself whose speciality of course was chemistry. There was also Guyton de Morveau, another chemist, who had started as a lawyer and educationist but who achieved eminence as a scientist. He had been a colleague of Lavoisier and had made history by ascending in a balloon at the battle of Fleurus in order to reconnoitre the enemy's lines. The mathematical sciences were directed by Joseph-Louis Lagrange who had held a chair in an artillery school at Turin. The students—386 of them—were recruited by competition from twenty-two cities in all parts of the Republic. They were required to furnish the usual proofs of *civisme*. According to the original regulation they had to be not less than sixteen years of age and not over twenty, but in the event the rule had to be relaxed. Among the 386 entrants seventy were over twenty, twenty-seven were younger than sixteen, and one was only twelve and a half. In addition to free instruction they received a maintenance grant of 1200 francs. They were boarded out in the families of suitable citizens, and not housed in an *internat*, as had been the usual custom in institutions of higher education. The college was lavishly equipped. There were laboratories, lecture-rooms, amphitheatres, all kinds of apparatus, models of machines and different kinds of boats, and specimens of chemical substances. There was plenty of practical work and the teaching was done largely by means of tutorials—a technique which at the time was something of a novelty. 'War', said Fourcroy, 'has become for the French people a fortunate opportunity for scientific development...By multiplying and inventing arts of defence hitherto unknown, by the aid of the geometrical and physical sciences, the Committee of Public Safety has recognised the importance of the sciences and the necessity of doing everything to apply them with industry and care.' The college proved an immediate success, but after less than a year of working it was decided to reduce somewhat the scope of its activities. In future it would specialise on work relating to military engineering, artillery, mining and naval constructions. At the same time, on 1 September 1795, the institution was renamed L'École Polytechnique; and in a modified form it has survived to the present day.

An even more immediate need than the training of military engineers was that of supplying the armies in the field with ammunition. In order to provide for the manufacture of arms and powder the Great Committee of Public Safety founded what it called L'École des Armes. On 2 February 1794 it was decreed that every district throughout the Republic should send two citizens, aged between twenty-five and thirty—i.e. just above the age for conscription—to Paris in order to take a course in the art of making gunpowder and forging cannon. It would last a month (three *décadis*), and the workers were to be paid three livres a day and would be lodged in a barracks. The end of the course was celebrated by a special festival at which the students exhibited samples of their work to the Convention and sang 'L'Hymne au Salpêtre'. Three courses in succession were organised and the whole scheme was supervised by a group of scientific specialists. For example, Fourcroy and Guyton de Morveau gave instruction in the manufacture of powder, and Hassen-fratz was in charge of the construction of cannons. It was hoped that the young men who had been trained in these short munition courses, when they returned to their own homes, would be able to inaugurate similar courses and so pass on their knowledge and experience. This would be a means of increasing the production of the ammunition that was so vitally needed. Their republican enthusiasm, it was felt, would compensate for any deficiencies in the meagre training which they had received. A somewhat similar scheme was inaugurated on 31 December 1794 for the institution of naval establishments at ports. Two candidates from every district in the country were to be trained in the equipment and repair of warships, in the handling of boats and in naval artillery. They also had part of their training actually at sea. This naval course lasted from February to November 1795.

But it was not only scientists and engineers or arms and ammunition that the Republic needed in its effort to ward off invasion by a coalition of the strongest nations in Europe. It was also necessary to train soldiers and provide officers to lead its armies in the field. Under the *Ancien Régime* there had been a number of attempts to found establishments with this end in view. In 1750, for example, an *école spéciale militaire* had been formed at La Flèche, and to it were added from time to time similar schools in various parts of France. But they were hardly professional schools like the St Cyr of later days or our own Sandhurst. They were more like the 'academies' of the seventeenth century which provided a 'modern' type of education, including mathematics and modern languages, and which gave attention to the use of arms, riding and courtly accomplishments. Their pupils were required to be of noble birth, and special arrangements were made for the sons of officers in poor circumstances. The schools of this type opened during the reign of Louis XV had for the most part been entrusted to the care of religious congregations—more particularly the Oratorians.[1] But

[1] From 1779 to 1784 Napoleon was a pupil at the military school at Brienne which was run by the Order of Minims. The *Encyclopaedia Britannica* (English edition), XIX, 190, says he afterwards used to speak 'with contempt' of the school and its staff; but Arthur Levy, in his *Napoléon intime* (Paris, 1892), pp. 30–2, adduces evidence to show that he had pleasant memories of his old school and maintained friendly relations with its staff.

in common with all establishments of that kind they had been suppressed in the early days of the Revolution, and others that remained were finally abolished, on a motion from Lakanal, by a decree of 2 September 1793. The only one still left was that of Auxerre. It was therefore a matter of urgency to make some provision for definitely military training.

The matter was raised in a report which Barère presented to the Convention on 1 June 1794. He claimed that the short emergency courses for training munition workers had proved successful and that a scheme on somewhat similar lines could be inaugurated in order to produce efficient soldiers. It had already been decided by the *levée en masse* that young men between the ages of eighteen and twenty-five should be con- scripted; but it seemed that, if a specialist training could be given to the group immediately preceding this, its members would be fitted when they were called up not only to serve in the army, but also if necessary to hold responsible positions in it. Even a course lasting only a few months would suffice to inspire them with patriotism, the hatred of tyrants and the practice of brotherhood; and they would also learn the art of warfare and have an opportunity, by physical exercises and a suitable régime, to accustom themselves to the rigours of a military life. The scheme was welcomed and supported in particular by Robespierre.

The new institution, which was to be called 'L'École de Mars', was of course to be quite unlike the military schools of the *Ancien Régime*. According to Barère, in order to be allowed entry to such establishments one had to be descended from 'some feudal brigand, some privileged scoundrel, some ridiculous marquis, some upstart baron or court hanger-on'. But the École de

Mars would be a purely republican institution, and poverty or misfortune would be a strong qualification for admission. The emphasis of the instruction would be practical. The cadets were to learn military drill, the use of the bayonet; the art of fortification and the details of military administration. They were to live under canvas and not in some imposing barracks 'built with the sweat of the people'. A sandy area—la plaine des Sablons—near Neuilly and not far from Paris, was chosen as the site of the camp and it was protected from intrusion from unauthorised persons by strong fences and chevaux de frise. It was decided that there should be three thousand cadets between the ages of sixteen and seventeen and a half. Six were to come from each district in the Republic and they were to be selected for their physical fitness and intelligence. They were to make their way from their homes to Paris on foot. A travelling allowance was granted and this was proportioned to the distance which had to be covered. There was a large response to the appeal for candidates and it is said that many of those who were not successful evinced their disappointment by bursting into tears. Most of the selected candidates arrived in Paris early in July 1794. They were exhorted to be not merely patriotic but to equal the Spartans in republican virtue and the Romans in courage, and also to sustain the honour of France against the 'crowned monsters'.

The life of the School was to be continually associated with those fêtes and ceremonies which were expected to kindle republican enthusiasm. For example, there was a solemn opening ceremony on 8 July 1794 when the cadets paraded before representatives of the Convention. They marched past to the sound of martial music and were commended for their enthusiasm and zeal.

'When the Republic has spoken republicans know no fatigue. A pure joy, a truly martial ardour—that is what we have seen displayed, and we have no hesitation in stating that the pupils of the camp of Les Sablons are already fit to give a lesson to the puppets of tyranny.' On 10 August, the fête in honour of the Constitution, there was a public display which took the form of a sham fight. The cadets, armed with bayonets and supported by cannon fire, stormed a redoubt which was manned by dummy figures among whom were represented the Pope, the Emperor of Austria, the Kings of England, Prussia and Spain, William Pitt and the Prince of Coburg. The cadets were encouraged to imitate the two young patriots Barra and Viala who had already become almost legendary heroes of the Revolution. The former was a youth of fourteen who had been killed by the Vendéeans, apparently for refusing to shout 'Vive le Roi!' Joseph-Agricole Viala also, who was only thirteen but already fired with republican zeal, had been shot during a skirmish near Avignon with some royalists who were on their way from Marseilles to Lyons.[1] In the centre of the camp at Les Sablons there was a building known as *la grande baraque*, in which lectures could be given and assemblies held. It was decorated with appropriate pictures and trophies of arms, and there was a platform at one end of it. At the back of this was a statue of Liberty, reaching up to the ceiling, and on either side were enormous busts of Barra and Viala who had been adopted as tutelary deities of the camp.

[1] In the Museum of the Institut Pédagogique National at Paris there are two eighteenth-century coloured prints, one depicting the death of Barra (HE. 12,433) and the other that of Viala (HE. 12,434). They are both celebrated in *Le Chant du départ*. The name Barra is sometimes spelt 'Bara'.

The cadets themselves were organised into three groups of 1000 each, and these were called *milleries*. Each was sub-divided into ten *centuries*, and each *centurie* into ten *décuries*. A soldier of experience commanded each *millerie*, and there were also officers for the other divisions. All the students alike wore a special uniform which had been designed by the painter David. It consisted of a blue tunic reaching to the knees and with red and white trimmings. There was a leathern belt fitted with slots in which to keep cartridges, gun-flints and other equipment. The red trousers were closely-fitting and ended in black leather boots which reached half-way up the thigh. Round the shoulders was a kind of scarf and a black shoulder-belt was also worn. On this were inscribed the words ÉGALITÉ. LIBERTÉ. On the head was carried a felt shako of the usual pattern with a tricolour cockade at the left side. The arms consisted of a short sword, a gun and bayonet for the foot-soldier and a lance for the cavalry-man. It was some little time before the whole complement of cadets could be fitted out with complete uniforms of this pattern. As far as underclothes were concerned, the equipment seems to have been rather meagre; only two shirts were allowed at first, though an extra one was issued on 7 August. The cadets were also allowed a tooth-comb and a button-hook.

Life in the École de Mars, as has been indicated, was certainly of a Spartan type. The daily ration of bread was strictly limited, and only twice in each *décadi* was fresh meat issued—salt pork was the fare on other days. From time to time fesh vegetables were made available. The normal drink was water, and in order to make it palatable it was customary to fortify it with vinegar. On special occasions a little wine was allowed. However, the cadets seem on the whole to have thrived on this régime. During the few months of the camp's existence only some 500 of the 3000 students needed any medical attention in the camp hospital, and there were only twelve deaths. The strict discipline and regular life doubtless contributed to this result. Reveille was at 5.0 a.m. and was announced by the firing of a cannon. Then followed a 'Hymne à l'Être Suprême' to the music of the camp band composed of young musicians. After this came instruction until 7.30, but the cadets had to wait till 9 a.m. before taking the first meal of the day. Then came various duties—e.g. going on guard or doing fatigues about the camp. That done, everyone repaired to the *grande baraque* where oral instruction was given, and this was followed by an hour and a half's recreation. Every three days a bathe in the Seine was permitted. The time of supper and of the evening exercises varied according to the season of the year, but the latter consisted mainly of drill and practice in the use of fire-arms. Another cannon at 7.30 p.m. announced the end of the day and everyone retired to his tent, but each cadet in turn had to form part of a patrol which went on guard duty during the night.

The course of instruction at the École de Mars, as it was finally organised, covered all aspects of the military art—drill, both of infantry and cavalry, and the use of arms including artillery. The various departments were in the hands of specialists under the general command of Florentin Bertèche, who had had a distinguished career in the revolutionary wars. For his heroic conduct at the battle of Jemappes (6 November 1792), in which he had been severely wounded, the Convention had voted him a crown of oak leaves.

In spite of the apparent success and efficiency of the

École de Mars and the attempt to kindle enthusiasm and republican patriotism among the cadets, there soon appeared signs of dissatisfaction. There were complaints about the rigours of camp-life, so different from the comforts of home which the students had only recently left behind. They felt themselves shut up in a kind of prison in which interviews even with parents had to be conducted across a fortified barrier and under the eyes of an official inspector. They complained of the crude and sometimes uneatable food which was supplied, and of their straw beds on the hard ground in the draughty tents. Appeals to the cadets by those in charge proved ineffective. After an impassioned address by a visiting representative of the Convention the only reply was 'Dans nos foyers'—'Let us go home'. At the time of Thermidor and the fall of Robespierre the camp had tended to split into two parties which reproduced the divisions in the Convention itself. There were even fights between moderates and extremists. An attempt to quieten the unrest was made by an assurance that the cadets would be sent back to their homes directly the course was ended, and it was obvious that the camp could not be maintained for taking further drafts of students. On 23 October 1794 Guyton de Morveau, speaking in the name of the Great Committee of Public Safety, claimed that in the short time that the École de Mars had been in existence it had proved that 'any soldier, whether infantry man or cavalryman, can learn in less than three months the use of arms and all the duties of his service, and how to carry out all types of manoeuvre with great precision'. He maintained therefore that the camp had already fulfilled its object. It was now time for the cadets to return to their own districts and there 'manifest an example of the virtues

which they have practised, and the quick results of
their training, and make these an object of emulation
among their compatriots; and, in a word, bring with
them that spirit of republican brotherhood which they
have derived from the School'. It was therefore decided
to close the École de Mars, and between 24 and 27
October the cadets returned to their homes. Their
expenses once more were paid and they were allowed
to keep their swords as a souvenir—also their three
shirts and a haversack; their other equipment had to be
returned to store. However, a deputation of them
remained behind and appeared before the assembled
Convention on 31 October in order to render a formal
vote of thanks on behalf of the members of the camp.
One of their number made a highly rhetorical speech.
'Fathers of the country, we are going far from you.
Deign to cast a paternal eye on your adopted children
who look forward eagerly to the opportunity of showing
their gratitude to you and to our native land.' A few of
the cadets stayed on in Paris and were admitted as
members of the École Polytechnique.

So ended the École de Mars. It had been a costly
experiment and had achieved little, although the
Convention, to save its face, tried to make out that it
had been a success. It is true none the less that many
of its ex-pupils distinguished themselves later in the
Napoleonic wars.

11 Écoles de santé. The Museum.
L'École Normale. Other écoles spéciales

There was yet another urgent need which the nation
had to supply. The exigencies of war call for the
services of soldiers and officers to lead them, as well as
of scientific specialists trained in military engineering
and the provision of armaments. But it is also necessary
to have surgeons and physicians to tend the wounded
in the field and to treat them in hospital. The next
matter therefore which the Convention had to consider
was the recruiting and training of an adequate supply
of doctors. Under the *Ancien Régime* there had been in
the country eighteen university faculties of medicine
and in most of the big towns there were guilds of
surgeons and apothecaries. There were also a number of
courses for midwives, but these women seem to have
been largely of the Mrs Gamp type and their educational
and professional standards were particularly low. 'The
dreadful ignorance of the midwives and their careless-
ness should make any sensible person anxious that our
wise legislators should put on end to a scourge which
affects especially our country districts. There it harvests
every year a large number of victims of the lack of skill
and charlatanism of the women who engage in this
work.'[1] Even the university medical curriculum was
largely bookish and formal, and it almost wholly
neglected the scientific and clinical studies which are
essential to a proper medical training. Although the
medical professors in charge were not lacking, it was

[1] *Archives Nationales*, F. 171004. Quoted by Duruy, *L'Instruction
publique de la Révolution*, p. 116.

said that in order to get any benefit from the course it was necessary to supplement the university teaching by taking private lessons with one or more of them. The universities were suppressed by a decree of 15 September 1793,[1] and although this measure was not immediately put into effect it left them in a state of suspended animation.

All this meant that in every part of the Republic the practice of medicine and surgery tended to be carried on by men who had had little or no systematic training and were mere empirics. But as war conditions spread and became more acute the need for skilled army doctors increased. Not only was there a shortage of them, but the mortality among those who were actually serving was alarming. Fourcroy reported to the Convention that more than six hundred *officiers de santé* had perished within six months during the exercise of their duties. 'But although the need for replacing them becomes every day more urgent, the means of doing so is lacking almost everywhere in the Republic. The schools of medicine have been shut since the suppression of the universities. Out of ten or a dozen schools of medicine which used to teach students there are scarcely two left, and they have lost most of their activity. The school at Paris is completely destroyed.'[2] On 4 December 1794, therefore, on the motion of Fourcroy it was decreed that three medical schools should be established 'designed to train medical officers for the service of army hospitals and of the navy'. These schools were to be situated at Paris, Montpellier and Strasbourg. Each district in the Republic was required to send a candidate, aged between seventeen

[1] See above, p. 125.
[2] See Duruy, *L'Instruction publique de la Révolution*, p. 118, n. 1.

and twenty-six, to one of them. The school at Paris was to have twelve professors and 300 students, and that at Strasbourg six professors and 100 students. The course in all three schools alike was to be both theoretical and practical, and was to embrace 'all branches of knowledge relating to the art of healing'. The new schools would also be closely associated with hospitals where plenty of clinical material would be available.

In order to provide the necessary preliminary training in science, courses were organised at the Jardin des Plantes. This establishment had been founded at Paris as the Jardin du Roi in 1626, but it was far more than the botanical school which its name might suggest. Even before the Revolution it had been associated with the teaching of medicine; and it was here, rather than in the University itself, that the student had a chance of some scientific training. Courses in chemistry, anatomy and surgery had been organised; but even so the resources were far from adequate, and similar institutions at Montpellier and some other French universities were equally ineffective. It was quite obvious that a complete re-organisation of medical training would be necessary in order to supply the urgent needs of the Republic at war. With this aim in view, therefore, on 10 June 1793 Lakanal, speaking in the name of the Committee of Public Instruction, had proposed that the Jardin des Plantes should be transformed into a huge scientific institution. There would be twelve chairs and some of them would be associated with the studies needed in a preliminary course—for example, general chemistry, applied chemistry, botany in the museum, botany in the field, two courses of zoology, human anatomy and the anatomy of animals. In order to indicate the scope of the work which this institution was to undertake it was decided to rename it the 'Museum of Natural History'; and to safeguard its republican character 'all the officers of the Museum alike shall bear the title of "professor" and enjoy the same rights. The office of director shall be abolished and his salary shall be divided equally among the professors'. Lakanal's proposal was accepted without debate and a month later the new institution came into being.

Another of the Convention's grandiose schemes was the formation of the École Normale for the professional training of teachers. The idea that teachers need some special preparation for their work was no new one in France. It is not always sufficiently realised that every Roman Catholic teaching congregation not only instructs pupils but also trains those who teach them. Methods and organisation in considerable detail are prescribed in specially prepared documents based on long experience and revised from time to time. Examples are the *Ratio Studiorum* of the Jesuits, the Ursulines' *Règlements* and De La Salle's *Conduite des écoles*. The congregations also provide considerable 'in service' training for their young teachers. From time to time actual training institutions had been formed in France. J. B. De La Salle had founded a 'séminaire de maîtres d'école' to prepare the Brothers of the Christian Schools for their calling; and in this work he had been fore-stalled by fourteen years on a smaller scale by Charles Demia who established the teaching congregation of Frères de Saint-Charles in the diocese of Lyons. If therefore the teaching orders were to be replaced by laymen, it would be necessary to provide for these latter some form of professional training such as that which the religious organisations had already ensured.

It was natural, then, that those who advocated a secular system of national education should be interested in the subject of teacher-training. As we have seen, Rolland had already included in his scheme the provision of 'une maison d'institution pour former des maîtres'. The whole issue was raised again in the Convention in a report read on 1 June 1794 by Barère in the name of the Great Committee of Public Safety. He proposed the establishment in Paris of 'a school in which teachers would be trained, so that they could afterwards be sent out into all the districts'. Five months later—on 30 October—Lakanal, speaking as a representative of the Committee of Public Instruction, proposed that there should be established in Paris a 'normal school' to which would be sent citizens who had already reached a satisfactory standard of education and who would there be instructed in the art of teaching by 'les professeurs les plus habiles dans tous les genres'. It was explained that the term 'Normale'[1] (from the Latin *norma* = 'rule') indicated that the new foundation was to be 'la type et la règle' of a number of similar schools which would be founded in various parts of the country.[2] The students would be selected by the administration of the various departments 'from the Pyrenees to the Alps', in the proportion of one to every 20,000 inhabitants. Candidates would have to be at

[1] The term *Normalschule* seems first to have been used by J. I. Felbiger, Abbot of Sagen in Silesia, who was an educational reformer in Germany and Austria, and who in 1774 was entrusted by Maria Theresa with the task of establishing teacher-training colleges. (See M. Gontard, *La Question des écoles normales primaires*, Toulouse, 1960, p. 5.)

[2] N.B. The École Normale of 1794 should not be confused with the École Normale Supérieure, for the training of secondary and higher teachers, which was founded in 1808. See below, p. 220.

least twenty-five years old and of good character and unquestioned patriotism. The course of training would last at least four months, and the expenses for travelling and during the course itself would be paid by the State. The Committee of Public Instruction would also take care to appoint as professors only 'citoyens qu'il croira les plus propres à remplir les fonctions d'instituteurs dans l'École Normale'. Their task would be to explain how the various subjects of the elementary curriculum should be taught; and at the end of the four months' course the students would return to their own districts, and there in their local *écoles normales* would pass on the training which they had received in Paris.

The scheme was debated and criticised, but it was finally adopted and the school actually came into existence. Some of the most eminent scholars and scientists of the day were recruited as professors. They included, for example, Lagrange, Laplace, Monge and Bernardin de Saint-Pierre. Their task was to impart to their students republican morality and the public and private virtues, as well as the techniques of teaching reading, writing, arithmetic, practical geometry, French history and grammar; and they were to use books which would be published and prescribed by the Convention. The work of the École Normale would be inspected and supervised by two representatives of the Convention. The course opened on 20 January 1795 and was held in the grand amphitheatre of the Museum. The students who had been selected numbered 1400. There was a fixed timetable; on the *primidi* and *sextidi* mathematics, physics and geometry were studied; on the *duodi* and *septidi*, natural history, chemistry and agriculture; on the *tridi* and *octidi*, geography, history and ethics; on the *quartidi* and *nonidi*, grammar, psychology and literature.

On the *quintidi* there was a discussion and the *décadi* was a holiday. The lectures given by the staff were taken down by shorthand-writers and afterwards published in a journal which was periodically distributed not only to the authorities of each district from which the students came, but also to agents of the French Republic in foreign countries.[1]

The fundamental weakness of the whole scheme was that the professors gave lectures which were directed towards the 'heights of science rather than towards the art of teaching'. This kind of instruction was of little value to those who for the most part would be concerned with the teaching of elementary subjects in primary schools. There seems also to have been little oversight of the students themselves. They were left free to make the most of their sojourn in the capital and to follow the course—or not—as they pleased. Thus the institution came under increasing criticism from certain members of the Convention and on the proposal of Daunou it was unanimously decided that the École Normale should be shut down on 19 May 1795. The students were allowed to return to their homes and the professors who had not finished their courses were permitted to do this in the pages of the journal to which reference has been made. Thus the experiment in itself proved a failure and the proposal to establish normal schools in the provinces was not carried out. But the principle that teachers need to be professionally trained and that the State is concerned in this business had been established; and it was destined to bear fruit in due course not only in France, but in other countries also.

[1] There is a first-hand report of some of the work of the École Normale in the *Moniteur* of 9 pluviôse III (29 January 1795).

The latter months of the Convention, after the excesses of Thermidor and the downfall of Robespierre, were marked by a series of educational developments the results of which, in many cases, still exist even if in a modified form. But there were two institutions which the Republic had inherited from the *Ancien Régime* and which managed to survive more or less intact in spite of the general destruction of educational establishments. One of them was the Collège de France. As was pointed out in chapter 1, this was a royal foundation and dated from the year 1530. It was a college of higher education, quite independent of the University of Paris, and had been much less hampered by tradition and much more accessible to the influences of the Renaissance. Its courses included mathematics and sciences, as well as literary subjects, and its motto was *Docet omnia*. For these reasons it was spared by the Revolution. Romme in his report of December 1792 had said 'There is one establishment which deserves to receive public attention because of its organisation which has been from time to time improved under François I, Henri IV and Louis XV, and because of the diversity and importance and utility of the instruction which it gives...It is the Collège de France which is too little patronised and which ought to be preserved.' Later, in the year 1801, Marie-Joseph Chénier, who had been deputy for the department of Seine-et-Oise during the Convention and a member of the Committee of Public Instruction, looking back on the record of the College, said 'The aim of this institution was to embrace the whole circle of knowledge...This excellent institution, in conformity with the principles of sound instruction which have characterised it from the beginning, has ever since perfected this by introducing new courses

156

and by continually improving methods of teaching. It deserves to outlive honourably those establishments which a fanatical adherence to routine has been able to preserve for so long'. So the College continued to function even during the period of the Terror, and from time to time it submitted to the Committee of Public Instruction a report on the plan and purpose of its courses. By a decree of 8 March 1793 it was decided that the salaries of its professors (now twenty in number) should be paid by the State, and on 13 July of the same year its title of Collège de France was officially confirmed. It remains today one of the chief establishments of higher education in France.

The other institution of the *Ancien Régime* which was not destroyed during the Revolution was the Bibliothèque Nationale. Founded as the Bibliothèque du Roi, it dated back to the time of Charles V in the fourteenth century. At the time of the Revolution it possessed 152,868 printed books. To these some 300,000 more were added; they had been confiscated from the libraries of suppressed ecclesiastical establishments and the houses of nobles who had emigrated. The plans of Talleyrand and Condorcet had envisaged incorporating the Bibliothèque Nationale in the general national educational system, and arrangements were made for it to be accessible to the general public.

The Convention also showed interest in various departments of higher technical education. Reference has already been made to the École Polytechnique and the écoles de santé which were successful and to the École de Mars and École Normale which were grandiose failures. But there were several other 'schools concerned with the different professions which are devoted to the service of the community and which demand special knowledge in the field of science and the arts'. Some reference must therefore be made to the more important of these.

There was, for example, the Conservatoire des Arts et Métiers. An engineer named Jacques de Vaucanson, who had invented machinery for the silk-industry at Lyons, had made a collection of machines and models of many kinds. When he died at Paris in 1782 he left this collection to the government. It thus formed the nucleus of a scientific museum, and additions were made to it from time to time. The Convention, by a decree of 11 February 1794, appointed a commission to be responsible for this collection and to add to it examples of agricultural and industrial machinery, and also to form a library of books and diagrams relating to these matters. The establishment was to be entitled Conservatoire des Arts et Métiers and three demonstrators were appointed in order to assist students who wished to work there. The Conservatoire thus acted as a supplement or reference department to the École Polytechnique. Another important aspect of its work was that it helped to replace the old system of apprenticeship which had been carried on under the *Ancien Régime* by the craft-guilds (*corporations*). These had been abolished by law, if not in fact, in 1791, and the whole system was in a state of chaos. In 1803, however, an attempt was made to regulate it through the medium of a Chambre des Arts et Manufactures—apparently with no great measure of success. But the Conservatoire itself survived the Revolution and was greatly developed during the nineteenth century. It still exists.

Something should also be said here about the École des Mines. In 1783 Louis XVI had formed a Corps des Ingénieurs des Mines, and a School of Mining was opened in Paris. The decree relating to this stated that the King realised the need for such a school in order to encourage the exploitation of mines which was proving of so great importance in other countries. He had therefore determined to establish an École des Mines on the lines of the École des Ponts et Chaussées which dated from 1747. Two professors were appointed and the course of instruction which included practical work —carried out sometimes in Germany—lasted three years. The School of Mining was re-established by the Convention in 1794. It was suppressed under the Consulate and re-opened in 1816. It also still exists.

Another interesting foundation was the Bureau des Longitudes. In the reign of Louis XIV an observatory had been founded in Paris and it soon acquired a considerable reputation; but by the middle of the eighteenth century its importance had declined and attempts to improve it had not proved very successful. But on 25 July 1795 Grégoire put forward a proposal which was immediately accepted. It was to the effect that a Bureau des Longitudes should be established which would have the direction of the Paris Observatory. It was also instructed to investigate and report upon the other observatories in the country which still existed, and to make recommendations to the Committees of Marine and of Public Instruction as to further establishments of the same kind which might still be needed. Another of its duties was to correspond with observatories in foreign countries. It was to publish calendars and astronomical tables and issue reports on astronomical and meteorological observations. Every year one of the members of the Bureau was to give a course of lectures on some aspect of astronomy or geography or map-making. The Bureau des Longitudes proved a great success and rendered valuable service. It is today the French meteorological office.

The Bureau des Longitudes was obviously designed primarily for the service of the navy which was of vital importance in the war against England which had been declared in February 1793; but there was also a subsidiary establishment for the benefit of the army. This was the École Nationale Aérostatique which was founded at Meudon by an order of the Committee of Public Safety made on 31 October 1794. Aeronautics had progressed considerably in France during the period just preceding the Revolution. The brothers Montgolfier had experimented with a hot-air balloon in June 1783, and the use of hydrogen as a lifting agent was successfully demonstrated by a physicist named Jacques-Alexandre-César Charles later in the same year. In October 1783 the first ascent by a human being was achieved by François Pilâtre de Rozier. The military value of the balloon was therefore soon recognised, as we have seen in the exploit of Guyton de Morveau at the Battle of Fleurus on 26 June 1794.[1] These events explain the formation by the Convention of a military school of aeronautics. It contained sixty students who were divided into two companies of *aérostiers*. The École Nationale Aérostatique, however, lasted only three years.

The Convention in its latter days not merely contented itself with encouraging institutions of higher scientific study and promoting research in science and its applications, but it also showed some interest in literary and aesthetic matters. Special mention should be made of the École des Langues Orientales Vivantes, which also had its forerunners under the *Ancien Régime*.

[1] See above, p. 138.

As far back as 1669 it had been decreed that every year six young Frenchmen should be sent to the Capuchin monasteries at Smyrna and Constantinople. There they were to study oriental languages for a period of three years and thus fit themselves to become interpreters in the 'Échelles du Levant'—the commercial ports of the Eastern Mediterranean with which Marseilles carried on a developing trade. During their course these 'jeunes de langue' were enjoined to make copies and translations of Arabic, Turkish and Persian texts; and these were to be deposited in the Bibliothèque du Roi. There had also been some teaching of oriental languages at the Collège de France and at the Jesuit college of Louis-le-Grand. A few boys from French families who were engaged in business in the Levant had been maintained at public expense in order to follow these courses. The commercial value of such instruction had therefore been demonstrated, and in 1790 an officer named Langlès called the attention of the Constituent Assembly to its importance and the dangers of its neglect. In the same year the Capuchins had offered to the Assembly a scheme for a parallel dictionary of the Armenian, Italian, Latin and French languages.

When therefore on 30 March 1795 Lakanal raised the subject of instruction in oriental languages he referred to their 'utilité reconnue pour la commerce et la politique'. The scholarships at Louis-le-Grand had of course lapsed with the expulsion of the Society of Jesus, and Lakanal said that there was a danger of this kind of instruction dying out. He therefore proposed the establishment of three courses at the Bibliothèque Nationale. They would deal with Arabic, Turkish, Crimean Tartar, Persian and Malay. This was agreed and three professors were appointed. Modern Greek was subsequently added to the curriculum. It was made clear that students were to confine their attention to the commercial aspects of these languages and that any kind of literary or archaeological research, such as might have been allowed or even encouraged under the *Ancien Régime*, was not to be permitted. 'Each citizen is responsible to the motherland for the whole of his time; he is not allowed to indulge in researches out of sheer curiosity at a time when the country is enjoying a stable peace and the late fruits of liberty. The researches that are needed nowadays are the routing out of traitors, and not the unearthing of monuments which have been hidden in the night of past ages.'[1]

In spite of this pronouncement the Convention had not always taken an exclusively utilitarian view of higher studies. This is evidenced by its provision for the preservation of antiquities and for archaeological research. On 4 June 1793 it passed a decree enforcing a penalty of two years' imprisonment against anyone who 'defaced *monuments des arts* belonging to national property'; and later in the same year it appointed a *commission des monuments* which was soon afterwards merged in a *commission des arts*. In January 1794 this body issued an 'instruction on the method of cataloguing and preserving, in all parts of the Republic, any objects which may be of value to the arts, sciences and education'. A collection of such material was also made and it constituted what in 1795 became the 'Musée des Petits Augustins'. This lasted until the Restoration in 1816.

A more permanent and important institution was the Conservatoire of Music. This was a development from the *Ancien Régime*. It dated from 1784, and in 1786 had

[1] See Hippeau, *L'Instruction publique*, II, 214.

been given the title of École Royale de Chant et de Déclamation Lyrique. It was largely concerned with training recruits for the opera. A school of music associated with the band of the Garde Nationale of Paris was incorporated with this institution, and on 3 August 1795 the combined establishment was opened under the title of 'Conservatoire de Musique'. Bernard Sarrette, who had been in charge of the National Guard band, was appointed its director and under him it rapidly developed. Although re-organised from time to time it has continued a successful career down to the present day and very many of the most distinguished French musicians have been associated with it. At the same time the pictorial arts were not neglected, and here again the Convention benefited by an inheritance from the *Ancien Régime*. In 1648 Louis XIV had founded an Académie des Beaux-Arts, and to this he added in 1671 an Académie d'Architecture. But in 1793 the Convention suppressed all academies, and it was for this reason that two years later it reconstituted and combined the two institutions in a single École des Beaux-Arts. Like the Conservatoire of Music, it has developed and flourished and has established an international reputation.

To sum up then, it was in the field of higher and professional education that the Convention made its most conspicuous and most lasting achievements. By the early nineteenth century France was the leading country in Europe in this respect. The French Institut and the École Polytechnique in particular stimulated the formation of similar institutions elsewhere[1]— notably in the new University of Berlin (1810). More normally, however, the French system of organising higher technical instruction in separate institutions

---

[1] Refer to *New Cambridge Modern History* (London, 1965), IX, 28.

apart from universities was until recent times very generally followed.

In passing it may be noted that the revolutionaries had abolished the universities in 1793 because they were 'corporations', like the craft-guilds (*corporations de métiers*) which had already been closed down in 1791. The assemblies distrusted all corporate institutions which suggested privilege and 'closed shop'; and the law passed in March 1791 had stated that anyone was to be 'free to carry on any business, profession, art or craft as he pleased'. But the university itself, as its name implies, was a guild or corporation, and its constitution and grades of membership had much in common with those of the medieval guild. The rebirth of the university as a corporate institution for the encouragement of scientific study, scholarship and research was largely a German phenomenon.[1] The French university faculties were certainly restored in 1808, but they remained under the direct control of the national government; and it was not until a reorganisation in 1896 that the faculties were grouped into corporate universities which were given a certain amount of autonomy and were encouraged to expand their courses of work.

Perhaps some reference should be made to an attempt on the part of the Convention to deal with the problems of handicapped children, though here the achievement was limited. A philanthropist named Valentin Haüy had interested himself in the education of the blind. In 1786 he published an *Essai sur l'éducation des aveugles* which set forth 'different methods, tested by experience, for enabling them to read by the aid of touch, and for printing books from which they can get a knowledge of languages, history geography, music, etc., and, perform

[1] See below, p. 243 n.

various kinds of work in connection with trades'. Haüy was in fact a forerunner of Braille, but apparently it was more in the performance of church music that his pupils distinguished themselves. The outbreak of the Revolution disorganised a society which had interested itself in the welfare of the 'jeunes aveugles' and had supported Haüy's work; but he made an appeal to the Constituent Assembly, and this body united the society's protégés with an establishment which had been founded for the benefit of deaf-and-dumb children. This had been started in pre-Revolution days by the Abbé de L'Épée, who was a distinguished pioneer in this kind of work. He died in December 1789 and was succeeded by another priest, the Abbé Sicard. By virtue of a law passed by the Constituent Assembly in July 1791 this school was declared to be an 'institution nationale'. When the École Normale was formed Sicard was included among its professors, and later he held a chair in the Institute. He was the author of a *Cours d'instruction d'un sourd-muet de naissance*.

In 1793 the combined institution catering for both blind and deaf-and-dumb children was re-organised by the Convention, but the object now was a purely utilitarian one—that of teaching handicapped children some kind of trade or accomplishment whereby they might be enabled to earn a living. The funds allocated to the school were insufficient to maintain it and it soon succumbed. However, L'Institution des Jeunes Aveugles was revived under more favourable auspices during the nineteenth century. At the Restoration in 1815 Sicard also was re-instated as director of the institute for the deaf-and-dumb, and his work there had important repercussions in other countries—especially England and the United States.

12 *Lakanal's law on primary education.*
The central schools. The Daunou law of 1795

In the last year of its existence the Convention once more turned its attention to the subject of primary education and to the organisation of a national system. Lakanal and Sieyès, who after the events of Thermidor had recovered much of their influence and were members of the Committee of Public Instruction, revived their scheme of June 1793 which had been set aside by the extremists. It was however presented in a somewhat modified form. For example, the clauses relating to national fêtes were cut out and so also was the proposal to establish a Central Commission for Public Instruction, for it was this that had roused most opposition from the Jacobins when the scheme was first put forward. The re-organised plan dealt mainly with primary education, and it was laid before the Convention of 16 November 1794 by Lakanal acting as president of the Committee of Public Instruction. There was a great deal of discussion and some opposition on the part of the 'montagnards'; but by this time this party formed only a minority in the Assembly, and on the following day (17 November) a 'Décret sur les Écoles Primaires' was adopted. Its chief provisions were as follows: Primary schools are to be established for children of both sexes, and they are to give the instruction needed by 'hommes libres'. Each school is to have two divisions—one for boys and one for girls— and therefore it must have both a master and a mistress. In all parts of the Republic there should be one school for every thousand inhabitants; but in sparsely and densely populated areas alike extra schools can be provided if the administration of the district thinks it advisable and the Assembly agrees. *Ci-devant* presbyteries can be used as school-houses and for the residence of teachers. The staff themselves are to be nominated by 'le peuple', but they will be examined, appointed and supervised by a special 'jury d'instruction' consisting of three members chosen by the district administration. The membership of this jury is to be renewed every six months, but re-appointment is permissible. All matters concerned with the appointment and dismissal of teachers or complaints against them will be the concern of this jury, or in the case of difficulty will be referred to the district authorities. 'All those who fulfil the honourable mission of instructing the children of the Republic are to be given the status of *fonctionnaires publics*.' They are to use text-books composed and published by order of the Convention and they are not allowed to take boarders or to give private lessons. Teachers' salaries are to be uniform throughout the country—1200 livres for masters and 1000 for mistresses; but a bonus is to be paid in areas which have over 20,000 inhabitants.

The decree goes on to deal with the curriculum and organisation of primary schools. Pupils must be at least six years of age before admission. The work of the boys' and girls' schools alike will comprise reading and writing; the French language both written and spoken; elementary arithmetic and land-measurement; some notions of geography and of the history of 'free peoples'; information about natural phenomena and products; stories of heroic deeds and 'chants de triomphe.' The reading material must inculcate republican principles, the Rights of Man and the French constitution. The teaching is to be in French, but if there is a local idiom it can be used as an auxiliary medium. Physical exercises are important because they promote health and agility. Boys are to be taught military drill. Swimming and various forms of athletics are prescribed. As in the 1793 proposal, pupils accompanied by their teacher and led by 'un magistrat du peuple' are to be taken on periodic visits to hospitals. Visits are also to be made to factories, industrial concerns and workshops, so that pupils may get some idea as to the sort of work to take up when they leave school. Children are to be encouraged to help in domestic and agricultural work and to assist the aged and the parents of 'defenders of their country'. Prizes are to be awarded every year on the 'fête de la jeunesse', and these celebrations will be attended by members of the public. The decree ends with an article declaring that any private citizen is free, if he wishes, to open an independent school, but it will be under the supervision of the public authorities. There is, however, no requirement that the teacher should possess a 'certificat de civisme'; and although he must give instruction in the Rights of Man and the constitution, there is no embargo on religious teaching in independent schools.

As will be seen and as has been said, this law was in large measure a repetition, with some omissions and amplifications, of the 1793 proposal; but in order to see that it was enforced the Convention on 18 November 1794 gave instructions to the Committee of Public Instruction that within a month a written report on the carrying-out of this law was to be submitted. It was to be drawn up under the following heads: the names of the communes where the primary schools will function; the date when each jury will be formed; when the masters and mistresses will be nominated; the names of communes where primary schools are still lacking; the reasons why they have not been provided; the names of citizens who have been invited by district administrations to serve on a 'jury d'instruction', but have declined to do so, and the reasons for their refusal. Other information required related to areas of very sparse population which would need primary schools; areas where school buildings were lacking, but no *ci-devant* presbytery was available; and any suggestions as to means of providing or improving primary schools. It was added that those juries which 'with a paternal solicitude' hasten to implement the law will be commended, whereas those which neglect to do so will be 'denounced to public opinion'.

On 16 December 1794 Lakanal once more presented a report on behalf of the Committee of Public Instruction,[1] but this time it dealt with secondary education. As far back as 1792 a Girondin deputy, Jean-Henri Bancal des Issarts, had put forward a proposal that in the chief town of each department there should be established an 'école centrale' to give a secondary education following on from that of the elementary schools. This suggestion was referred to the Committee of Public Instruction, but it was set aside for the time being. It was, however, now revived and it formed an important element in a scheme for a national system of education which the Convention ultimately adopted nearly three years later. But first of all came Lakanal's report. He tried to allay criticisms that the proposals outlined above would prove too expensive, and he asserted that one primary school to every two thousand inhabitants would be sufficient. From these schools pupils would be able to go direct to central schools

[1] Reprinted in Hippeau, *L'Instruction publique*, I, 423–45.

which would be founded on the ruins of the former *collèges*. It appears from this recommendation that some schools of this type were still managing to maintain a bare existence. The majority of pupils would, of course, leave the primary school to go into agriculture or industry. They would have 'found in the primary schools all that is necessary for them to fulfil with honour, in their various callings, their status as citizens...But for the glory of the motherland, for the advancement of human knowledge, it is necessary that young citizens who have been excepted by nature from the ordinary class should find a sphere in which their talents can be given scope.' It was for these select candidates that Lakanal's central schools were designed. There would be no need for any kind of intermediate secondary school. The central schools, said Lakanal, 'are not secondary schools. These have become redundant because of the scope which you have given to schools for young children. Primary schools, in fact, afford the germs of all the studies which will be taught in the central schools. Intermediate, district and cantonal schools would be superfluous'. The title *central* was to be given to Lakanal's schools because each would be the centre of a group of contributory primary schools and thus accessible to those who were qualified to attend them. There was little discussion on this proposal and it was adopted without opposition on 25 February 1795.

The chief provisions of the decree were as follows: There is to be one central school to every 300,000 inhabitants, distributed over the whole Republic,[1] and

[1] Normally the central school would be situated in the chief town of a department, but other towns could get authority to open an *école centrale supplémentaire*. There is a good account of such a school in M. Lebrun, *Histoire du Collège de Pontoise, 1564–1922* (Paris, 1923), pp. 81–4.

the curriculum will embrace the sciences, letters and arts. The age-range of the pupils will be from eleven or twelve to seventeen or eighteen. Every school is to have one professor for each of the following subjects: mathematics; experimental physics and chemistry; natural history; scientific method and psychology; political economy and legislation; the philosophic history of peoples; hygiene; arts and crafts; general grammar; belles lettres; ancient languages; the modern languages most appropriate to the locality of the school; painting and drawing. The teaching throughout will be in French. Every month there is to be a public lecture dealing with the latest advances in science and the useful arts. Every central school is to have attached to it a public library, a garden and a natural history collection, as well as a collection of scientific apparatus and of machines and models relating to arts and crafts. The Committee of Public Instruction is to remain responsible for the composition of text-books which are to be used in central schools, and the siting of these schools is to be determined by special enactment.

The second part of the decree deals with the staff of these schools. Teachers will be appointed and supervised by a 'jury central d'instruction' nominated by the Committee of Public Instruction. Their annual salaries are fixed provisionally at 3000 to 5000 livres according to the population of the area which the school serves. A grant of 6000 livres is also to be made every year to each school in order to cover the expenses of the library and other equipment; and the Committee of Public Instruction is ultimately responsible for seeing that these regulations are carried out. The school itself will be run by a committee of teachers, meeting every *décadi*, and its finances will be the concern of the departmental administration. Primary school pupils who are most distinguished will be granted by popular vote, and at the *fête de la jeunesse*, an annual bursary which will entitle them to a free place in a central school. The teachers of such successful pupils will be awarded a civic crown. In virtue of this law on central schools all still-existing colleges maintained at public expense in any part of the Republic are to be closed; and the Committee of Public Instruction is directed to make a report on existing scientific institutions, botanical gardens, collections of natural history, observatories, and societies which should be preserved and incorporated in this new scheme of education.

In order to hasten the establishment of both primary and central schools the Convention decided on 17 April 1795 to send round five commissioners of whom Lakanal was one. Their findings[1] revealed the great deficiency in particular of primary schools and the lack or incompetence of teachers—'people of ability have almost all perished and we have fallen into a state of dreadful barbarism'. To finance a satisfactory system of public instruction would be a costly business, but Lakanal believes that the estimate can be reduced and he explains methods of doing this. He envisages a total national educational expenditure of 25,856,000 livres. The greater part of this will of course be devoted to the primary and central schools, but provision is also made for the special schools of higher education. 'The results which this estimate reveals ought to destroy completely the exaggerated idea of the cost of public instruction which seems to be held; and this expense ought to diminish day by day because of the saving on the preliminary equipment.'

[1] See Hippeau, *L'Instruction publique*, I, 470–86.

Meanwhile the Convention was nearing the end of its career, and a new constitution was to take the place of that which had been enacted in 1793, but never properly put into practice. The franchise was made dependent on the payment of taxes, and this put political power into the hands of the nouveau-riche bourgeoisie. The advisability of a bicameral system of government had become apparent, and legislative power was therefore entrusted to two Chambers—that of the Five Hundred, which had the power to initiate laws, and that of the two hundred and fifty 'Ancients' whose approval was necessary before they could be passed. The executive power was given to five Directors, one of whom was to retire each year. They were to be chosen by the Chambers and were responsible to them. This new constitution had been drawn up by a Commission des Onze—a committee of eleven members of whom Daunou was one. They did not neglect the subject of public instruction. A separate section (*Titre* X) of the Constitution of the Year III (1795) deals with this. 'There are', it says, 'in the Republic primary schools where the pupils learn reading, writing, and the elements of arithmetic and ethics. The Republic provides the cost of housing the teachers who have chargeof these schools. There are also in various parts of the Republic schools higher than the primary schools, and their number shall be such that there will be at least one in every two departments. There is for the whole Republic a National Institute designed to record discoveries and perfect the arts and sciences. There is no system of subordination or administrative dependence among the various establishments of public instruction. Citizens have the right to open private establishments of education and instruction, as well as independent societies designed to encourage the progress of the sciences and the arts.'[1] One of the very last acts of the Convention was to approve a report drawn up by Daunou and amplifying *Titre* X of the Constitution. It covered the whole system of public instruction. This was presented on 25 October 1795, the day before the Convention dissolved itself; and the scheme was therefore left to the Directory to be carried out.

The Daunou law is important and interesting because it is a kind of summary of the educational projects and experiments which had been made ever since the Revolution first broke out. As we have seen, modifications and deletions were made from time to time, but there is a family likeness about the various schemes which were put up from Mirabeau's proposals onwards. Throughout there is the same opposition to traditional curricula and methods, and to any kind of ecclesiastical control of education, the same belief in the State's responsibility for it, and the same enthusiasm for the inculcation of republican principles. The scheme for public instruction introduced by Daunou and which became law on 25 October 1795 incorporated the primary schools which Lakanal had sponsored in the previous November, and also the central schools which he had more recently advocated. It included and extended the special and professional schools to which some reference has already been made. Thus the Daunou scheme comprises three stages, each of which had been adumbrated by previous legislation.

The first part of his *Loi sur l'organisation de l'instruction publique* deals with primary schools. There is to be one in every canton, which in the Constitution of 1795

---

[1] F. Boursin and A. Challamel, *Dictionnaire de la Révolution française* (Paris, 1893), p. 916.

had replaced the commune as the basic unit of administration. The effect therefore would be to set up primary
schools in town centres of population and leave villages
and areas of scattered population unprovided. The
curriculum, organisation and equipment are to be in
accordance with Lakanal's scheme, and each school
will have two divisions, one for boys and one for girls.
This means that it will have both a school master and
a school mistress. Fees, fiixed by the departmental
authorities, are payable, but a quarter of the pupils
may be exempted on grounds of poverty. The second
section of the law is concerned with the central schools.
The provisions of the February 1795 decree were
included more or less as they stood, but the professors
of scientific method and of hygiene have disappeared.
The unit of school organisation is not the class, but the
course. There are to be ten separate courses arranged in
three sections. In the first are grouped drawing, natural
history, ancient and modern languages; in the second,
mathematics and experimental physics and chemistry;
in the third general grammar, belles lettres, history and
legislation. To be admitted to the first section the pupil
must be at least twelve years of age, to the second
fourteen, and to the third sixteen. There is no upper
age-limit for leaving school. Here again a quarter of the
pupils may be given free places if they are unable to
pay fees.

The third part of the Daunou law is concerned with
higher professional and technological education. The
provision of special schools dealing with the following
subjects is prescribed: astronomy; geometry and
mechanics; natural history; medicine; veterinary art;
rural economics; antiquities; political science; painting,
sculpture and architecture; music. There are also to be

schools for those born blind and for the deaf-and-dumb. As has been shown, many of such institutions were already in existence and would be incorporated in this general educational scheme. It was also decided that existing schools for civil and military engineering, artillery and naval services should be maintained. It was all to be severely practical. 'In the special schools the sciences will be more reasonably and less fanatically regarded. Altars will not be erected to them, but the benefits which accrue from them will be appreciated. They will no longer be regarded with superstition, but with gratitude. In short, one cannot overestimate the happy results of a system which would keep the sciences and arts closely related and, by causing them to react one on the other, would conduce to progress and utility.'

Finally, the law of October 1795 provided for a National Institute of the Sciences and Arts which harks back to the original plans of Condorcet and Talleyrand. Its aim will be to promote research and publish the results of this, and also to correspond with learned societies in other countries. In this way it will benefit the State and glorify the national reputation. It was designed as a substitute for the former academies which had been situated in towns all over the country and were independent of one another. It would replace them by an organised centre of information and research covering all departments of human knowledge; it has been said that 'the Institute was born and the *Encyclopédie* became alive'. With this end, therefore, it was divided into three main sections, and each section in turn contained several different classes. The first section embraced mathematical and scientific subjects, and included medicine and rural economics; the second was devoted to moral and political sciences, together with history and geography; while the third was concerned with literature and the beaux-arts. The Institute was to comprise 144 members living in Paris and an equal number from the departments, together with twenty-four associate members from foreign countries. Each member would be required to identify himself with one particular section, but he would be free to attend meetings of other sections if he wished to do so. Four times a year there was to be a general meeting in which all sections would combine, and the proceedings of the Institute would be published regularly.

As has been said, the Convention ceased to exist on the day following that on which the Daunou law of 25 October 1795 was passed, and it was left to the Directory and subsequent governments to implement at any rate in some form and to some extent the inheritance which had been passed on to them. On 6 December 1795 forty-eight members, forming one-third of the full complement of the Institute, were nominated by the government, and they assembled under the chairmanship of Benezech, who was Minister for the Interior. They proceeded to co-opt ninety-six more members so as to bring the total up to the full number assigned to the city of Paris. Those chosen were then allotted to the various sections and an inaugural session was held with due pomp and ceremony on 4 April 1796. Thus the Institute got under way. It was at first installed in the Louvre, but in 1806 it was transferred to the building which had housed the Collège des Quatre Nations, founded by Mazarin in 1661. After the passing of the Civil Constitution Act in 1790 the college had continued to be carried on by an 'assermenté' staff, and then for a time it housed an *école centrale*. When the Institute was moved to this site its organisation was modified and again under the Restoration; but in spite of subsequent developments it survives to the present day with its five constituent academies. It may be regarded as the outstanding educational achievement of the Revolution period.

13 *Independent schools under the Directory.*
   Development of the central schools

The Daunou law of 25 October 1795 was undoubtedly
one of the most important pieces of educational legislation passed during the Revolution period because,
unlike some of its predecessors, it was to some extent
at any rate put into effect. As has been pointed out, the
existing primary schools were incorporated into the
system; but in spite of Lakanal's law, there was no
attempt to regulate their number according to the size
of the population which they had to serve, as had been
done in former schemes. Instead the supply of such
schools was left to be determined by the administration
of the individual canton. Instruction was not to be free,
except in cases of poverty, nor was it made obligatory.
The oversight of the schools and the appointment of
staff were ultimately the responsibility of the local
authorities acting through a 'jury d'instruction'. But
in many cases these bodies were little interested in
educational matters or competent to deal with them,
and the result was that even after the passing of the
Daunou law some cantons remained unprovided with
'State' schools. For example, as late as the year 1798
fourteen of the cantons in the department of Jura had
no such primary schools. In the Bas Rhin out of 366
arrondissements only 115 had such schools. Lack of
suitable teachers was one of the chief reasons for the
deficiency. Their remuneration, although paid by
parents and fixed by the departmental authorities,
meant very little in fact owing to the 'discrédit du
papier monnaie'—i.e. the *assignats* in which fees were

paid.[1] The result was that teachers were often 'discouraged by the great distress in which they were plunged'. Although, as in former education laws, the teacher was supposed to be provided with a house and garden, such accommodation was not always available owing to *ci-devant* ecclesiastical property having already been sold. The teacher-shortage is illustrated by appeals 'aux patriotes français des deux sexes'. For example, in the department of Finisterre an advertisement issued by the *jury d'instruction* of the district of Quimperlé 'invites all those of both sexes who are willing to fulfil, within the limits of its jurisdiction, the functions of schoolmaster or schoolmistress to report to them as soon as possible. They should be provided with a certificate of good conduct furnished by the general council of the commune in which they live, and which will attest that the candidate is not given to intemperance. Without these qualifications no candidate will be admitted to the interview'.[2] One is reminded of somewhat similar advertisements put out by local authorities in our own day, though the reference to dissolute habits is fortunately no longer appropriate.

Primary schools were also still hampered by a lack of suitable text-books. It was complained that those provided by the government could be used in central schools, but were not adapted to elementary instruction. Another obstacle to the development of primary education was the opposition of many parents to the anti-religious attitude of the 'State' schools, as well

[1] In October 1795 the number of *assignats* which could be purchased for 24 livres in cash was 1205. (See *Cambridge Modern History*, 1904 edition, VIII, 709; and refer also to the graph in F. Finet and R. Richet, *La Révolution*, 2 vols (Paris, 1966), II, 97.)

[2] This advertisement is reproduced in L. Tarsot, *Les Écoles et les écoliers* (Paris, 1893), p. 181.

as the negligence or incompetence on the part of local authorities to which reference has been made.

During the period of reaction after the events of Thermidor there had been a considerable development of independent schools, run in many cases by ex-ecclesiastics whose attitude towards religious teaching and republican 'morality' was more in accordance with what parents desired. The movement was also encouraged from outside by bishops who had emigrated. For example, Asseline the ex-Bishop of Boulogne, speaking at a meeting of priests exiled in Germany, said 'Ministers who have a cure of souls will exert themselves to the utmost to procure for their children a catholic education...They will stimulate the zeal of parents in this respect and attempt to find in every canton pious persons who will undertake this good work'.[1] By a decree of 5 February 1798 the Directory made an attempt to cope with this type of competition with the 'State' schools. Its aim was to provide supervision of private establishments. It was hoped 'to arrest the progress of the baneful principles which a host of private teachers are striving to implant in their pupils. The government ought not to neglect any means in its power to promote and encourage republican instruction.' To this end cantonal administrations are commissioned to visit, at least once a month and without previous notice, all *pensionnats* and private schools in their areas. They are to make sure that teachers base their instruction on the Rights of Man and the French Constitution, and that they are using the text-books which had already been prescribed by the Convention. They are also to see that the schools observe the *décadis* and the republican festivals, and that the conditions

[1] Jean-René Asseline, *Œuvres choisies* (6 vols, Paris, 1823), I, 123.

under which the children are taught are healthy and suitable. Any private schools which do not conform to these conditions are to be closed, but previous notice is to be given to the departmental administration. This kind of legislation, however, does not seem to have been very successful in checking the growth or controlling the running of independent schools. In April 1799, for example, in the department of Doubs there were 336 private schools and only 90 'State' ones. In the department of Sarthe 'the cantons contain "little schools" where they teach moral theology . . . They are supported by fanaticism and are impenetrable to the eye of the public official'. Quotations to this effect could be greatly multiplied.[1]

An interesting and outstanding example of an independent boarding-school for girls was the institution at Saint-Germain founded by Mme Campan in 1794. She had been *femme de chambre* to Marie Antoinette and we owe to her some valuable memoirs on the private life of Louis XVI's unfortunate queen. The school was modelled on Mme de Maintenon's Maison Royale de Saint-Cyr.[2] A fairly wide curriculum was adopted and it included games, and physical exercises, as well as music and dancing. The girls did their own housework. Stress was laid on religious instruction and Mme Campan even ventured to run a school chapel and appoint a chaplain. The authorities showed some hostility to the institution, and when the headmistress tried to protest to the visiting inspectors she was told 'Citizeness, you argue in the old-fashioned way. No reasons, please. When the Nation has spoken we require

---

[1] See, for example, A. Babeau, *L'École de village pendant la Révolution*, pp. 144–66.

[2] See H. C. Barnard, *Madame de Maintenon and Saint-Cyr* (London, 1934), *passim*.

obedience and not clever remarks'. However, by 1797 the situation had eased somewhat and Mme Campan was able to re-open her chapel and resume teaching her pupils stories from the Bible. When in 1808 Napoleon established a school at Écouen for the daughters of members of the Legion of Honour, Mme Campan was put in charge of it. Two of his sisters, Pauline and Caroline Bonaparte, had been pupils at Saint-Germain.

The Directory's opposition, then, seems to have been directed mainly against private schools in which the old Roman Catholic doctrines were taught. There was less objection to religious teaching of a vaguer kind which could be more easily reconciled with the political and philosophical outlook of the Revolution. Some reference in this connection should be made to the movement called 'Theophilanthropy' which had educational, as well as religious, implications. It had originated in England. A dissenting minister named David Williams,[1] who was a disciple of Locke and Rousseau, had founded in London a club at which religion based on reason rather than on revelation was discussed. Benjamin Franklin was among its members. In 1776 Williams opened a chapel near Cavendish Square and started Sunday services at which he used a liturgy composed by himself and based on 'the universal principles of religion and morality'. He got into touch with Voltaire who approved of his ideas and made them known in France. At a session of the Legislative Assembly held on 26 August 1792 David Williams was

[1] See A. Mathiez, *La Théophilanphropie et la culte décédaire* (Paris, 1904), and N. Hans, *New Trends in Education in the Eighteenth Century* (London, 1951), pp. 163–5. There is a good account of David Williams' work in England in W. A. C. Stewart and W. P. McCann, *The Educational Innovators* (London, 1967), pp. 35–52.

given the honorary title of *citoyen français* along with several other distinguished foreigners, including Tom Paine, William Wilberforce, Jeremy Bentham and George Washington. Theophilanthropy owed something to the vague deism of some of the eighteenth-century French philosophers, something to utilitarianism, and something to freemasonry. It acknowledged the existence of God and the immortality of the soul, and it celebrated festivals in honour of such divers characters as Socrates, St Vincent de Paul, Rousseau and George Washington. One of the French theophilanthropists, named Daubermenil, even established a ritual in which a perpetually burning fire was regarded as a symbol of the Deity.

David Williams himself had been greatly interested in education and had written several treatises on it; and in France the theophilanthropic movement from the beginning was associated with schools. In 1796 the Directory, recognising that the cult was in sympathy with republican theories and was not unlike the worship of Reason and of the Supreme Being, placed twenty churches in Paris at the service of the sect, and others were opened in some provincial towns—e.g. Dijon, Rouen, Sens and Château-Thierry. In connection with them schools were opened, and in these children were taught not only the usual academic subjects, but also 'whatever one owes to God, to one's parents, to one's country, to all mankind and to oneself'. Specially composed textbooks, such as *Le Manuel des théophilanthropes ou adorateurs de Dieu et amis des hommes* (Paris, 1797), were prescribed. However, the sect soon fell into disfavour with the government. In October 1801 it was formally suppressed. The churches were closed and with them the schools disappeared.

The most interesting, and perhaps the most important, part of the Daunou law of October 1795 was that which created the central schools. In order that the Directory might carry out the requirements of the decree it was first of all necessary to provide buildings for the new schools. Any still-available former *collège* premises could be utilised, and, as in the case of primary schools, *ci-devant* ecclesiastical property and former residences of émigrés were requisitioned for this purpose. For example, the *école centrale* of the Department of Oise was located in what had been an Ursuline convent, while that of Ariège was started in a château. If there were not sufficient buildings of this type available it was decided by an act of 13 July 1796 that the departmental administration was to be responsible for finding suitable accommodation. So by and large the Daunou scheme for central schools got started, though it took nearly a year to put it into effect. However, at the 13 July session Fourcroy was able to say 'Ninety central schools seem suddenly to have sprung up from nothing and to be supplanting the colleges in which barbarous methods have done nothing more than repeat for years on end the elements of a dead language'.[1]

In order to foster the central schools and discourage the growth of independent schools it was enacted by a law of 17 November 1797 that 'citizens who are not married and not serving in the army, if they wish to obtain any kind of administrative post under the Government, must submit with their application a birth certificate and also proof that they have attended

---

[1] See Hippeau, *L'Instruction publique*, ii, 241. In *Vie de Henri Brulard* (chap. xxiii) Stendhal gives a description of the *école centrale* at Grenoble where he was a pupil from 1795 to 1799.

one of the Republic's schools'. If the candidate was married and had children of school age he had to supply evidence of the same kind in respect of them.[1] The effects of this law were widely felt. For example, 'it sent children and parents alike crowding into these schools. At Paris you could see old clerks, aged fifty to sixty, who were compelled to attend the central schools in order to qualify for the certificate which entitled them to preserve their jobs or to obtain new ones'.[2] Through means like this the central schools were kept alive and by the middle of 1798 their number had risen to ninety-seven and an annual budget of some 3,500,000 francs had been allotted for their upkeep.

It should be noted, however, that these schools took the place of 562 colleges, giving a secondary education, which had been in existence in 1789. Moreover, many of them were already in difficulties. The recruitment of staff, as in the case of the primary schools, was a perpetual problem, and the Daunou law had made no provision whatever for the training of teachers. A large proportion, therefore, of central school staff had originally been serving in pre-Revolution colleges, but had since fulfilled republican requirements. At the *école centrale* at Lyons, for example, nine of the twelve professors came in this category. Yet it is true that some of the central schools attained a measure of success—especially those in the capital and in some of the large towns such as Nantes, Bourges, Metz, Nancy, Besançon, Toulouse and Montpellier. At Paris, where it had been decided that there should be five central schools, three were actually opened—those of the

[1] The text of the decree is given in Duruy, *L'Instruction publique de la Révolution*, pp. 180–1.
[2] Quoted in Louis-Grimaud, *Histoire de la liberté d'enseignement*, ii, 333–4.

Quatre Nations and of the Panthéon, and one in the Rue St Antoine which today is the Lycée Charlemagne. These schools had succeeded in attracting some distinguished scientists and scholars on their staffs. The salary of the teachers in these Parisian *écoles centrales* was fixed at 3000 francs a year, plus a capitation fee of twenty-five francs per pupil.

One of the disadvantages under which most of the central schools (and especially those in the provinces) laboured was that, unlike the old colleges, they did not provide an *internat* for the accommodation of boarders. At Paris, however, there still existed some *pensionnats* which, as in the case of the private schools, were run by ex-ecclesiastics or former teachers in the colleges of the University. They sent their older pupils to one of the *écoles centrales* and helped them with their homework. For example, some of the colleges of the ancient University of Paris had managed to exist in a more or less maimed condition during the earlier years of the Revolution.

One of the chief of these, the ex-Jesuit College of Louis-le-Grand, continued to function under the title of Collège Égalité. When the Marseillais arrived in Paris in 1792 they had been lodged in its buildings, and soon afterwards part of it was converted into a prison. However, such pupils as it managed to retain acquired a reputation for patriotism and many of them afterwards distinguished themselves in the Republican armies. On the other hand students seem sometimes to have been infected with the spirit of the times and to have interpreted the catch-words 'liberty' and 'equality' in terms of indiscipline. Such, for example, was the member of the Collège des Quatre Nations who pinned an indecent inscription on the coat-tails of a distinguished visitor.

When the central schools were instituted the pupils of the Paris schools, who had been granted free places and given the name of 'élèves de la patrie', were housed in the Collège Égalité which in 1798 changed its name to 'Prytanée française'. The pupils were sent for their lessons to the nearest central school which was that of the Panthéon. Similarly the former college of Sainte-Barbe, under a progressive principal named Lanneau de Marey, became the Collège des Sciences et des Arts. It had seven graduated classes, on the lines of those of the *Ancien Régime*, and the youngest pupils were taught in the college itself. The older ones, like those of the Collège Égalité, attended courses at the Panthéon central school. Arrangements of this kind were also made in some of the provincial towns. In a speech delivered in April 1800 Fourcroy, looking back, was able to say 'Since the suppression of the colleges and the universities the former schools have taken on a new lease of life, and a large number of private establishments have been formed for the education of youth. I could give as praiseworthy examples among private establishments, whether old or new, the schools of Sorèze, of Juilly and of La Flèche,[1] and the *pensionnats* of Évreux, of Fontainebleau, and of Metz—and several others'.

It can be safely said that, with the exception of the three Parisian schools and those in a few provincial towns, such as those which have been mentioned, the *écoles centrales* were only a qualified success. This was due not only to the disabilities already indicated, but in

[1] The Collège de Sorèze was a Benedictine foundation dating from 757. Juilly was one of the chief Oratorian establishments (see H. C. Barnard, *The French Tradition in Education*, pp. 158–72). The school at La Flèche apparently refers not to the famous Jesuit College which was closed in 1762, but to a 'military school' founded there in 1764 and directed by Doctrinaires.

many cases to the attitude of the local prefect—whether he were co-operative or hostile or merely negligent. Also the very organisation and curriculum of the schools themselves left much to be desired. One of the basic weaknesses was the replacement of classes by courses. Instead of a graduated curriculum a series of unrelated courses, each lasting as a rule two years, was substituted. Moreover, within the courses themselves there was no coherence or co-ordination. For example, pupils from twelve to fourteen could study drawing, natural history and ancient languages; but at the age of fourteen they would normally be switched on to mathematics and experimental science. After two years of these subjects they would go back to general grammar, literature and history. Moreover—and it is important to note this— the subjects in each course were optional. Pupils could take them or not as they pleased and there was no prescribed scheme of work or source of advice on what subjects to choose, unless the teachers concerned voluntarily undertook this. The result was that there were great differences in the number and standard of attainment of the pupils in the various groups, and proper 'streaming' was difficult and often impossible. The following statistics, taken more or less at random, for the years 1798 or 1799, give some idea of the numbers in the groups in some central schools. The list (shown on p. 190) includes examples both of the most successful and the least successful ones.

These examples illustrate the fact that, owing to the enormous variations, averaging the number of pupils in the different courses may give a misleading idea of the real state of the central schools. For example, Albert Duruy, analysing the courses taken by pupils in fifteen central schools selected from various parts of

Central school	Section I (minimum age of entry 12)			Section II (minimum age of entry 14)		Section III (minimum age of entry 16)			
	Drawing	Nat. hist.	Languages	Maths.	Phys. and chem.	Gen. gram.	Belles lettres	Hist.	Legis.
Besançon (Doubs)	221	18	53	159	37	33	20	38	42
Tours (Indre et Loire)	102	27	13	49	21	3	10	14	7
Chârtres (Eure et Loir)	52	0	43	10	15	20	0	0	0
Pau (Basses Pyrénées)	40	2	10	39	0	7	9	5	6
Agen (Lot et Garonne)	61	4	5	18	10	5	0	0	0
Soissons (Aisne)	20	7	8	7	0	0	0	0	0
Châteauroüx (Indre)	10	0	7	7	0	0	3	0	0

France, points out that an average of 89 pupils were taking drawing, 28 mathematics, 24 ancient languages, 19 natural history, 19 physics and chemistry, 15 general grammar, 10 history, 8 legislation and 6 belles lettres; but the fifteen schools include two of the most flourishing —those of Toulon and Besançon—and these tend to expand the statistics and conceal the fact that in many cases the central schools were poorly attended and that some of the courses had no pupils at all. It looks as if drawing were chosen by so large a proportion of pupils almost everywhere because it was a 'soft option'; but another reason probably is that with mathematics and science subjects it formed a suitable training for entry into the École Polytechnique. The whole curriculum, however, seems very extraordinary to a modern critic.

Some idea of the subsequent history of the central schools can be gathered from a report which was made to the Minister of the Interior, François de Neufchâteau. The Convention had suppressed ministries in order to get the powers of government more directly into its own hands; and it had replaced them by executive commissions, such as that on Public Instruction from which so many educational projects had emanated. One of the first acts of the Directory was to restore the ancient ministries, and the one concerned with public instruction was that of the Interior. This arrangement was continued under the Consulate. The official under the Minister, who dealt with this department, was entitled 'directeur de l'instruction publique', and he was assisted by a small council of experts. This council had been instructed in October 1798 to inquire into a report upon the state of the central schools throughout the country—'the hopes and fears that may be raised in reference to them, and the improvements which it may be possible to make in them without upsetting this huge machine which has been brought into being'. Thus the report,[1] which was issued on 5 February 1800, gives a picture of the central schools after five years of working—'L'état au vrai de l'instruction publique en France'.

It was based on information which had been supplied by the administrative authorities concerned and also by individual teachers. It refers first of all to the text-books which had been prescribed and which were being used in central schools; and it says that on the whole they can be relied upon to 'inspire young people with sound, liberal and philosophic views'. It goes on to say that, all the same, the crucial matter is the way in which the books are used and the subjects are taught; and it summarises the replies which it has received from teachers on this point. The course in drawing, as has been indicated, is the most popular. For example, in the central school at Montpellier no less than 348 pupils are taking this subject. It appears, however, that often in practice drawing was not limited to the two years of the first section, but that it was 'séparé de la chaine des études'. Many of the pupils who chose this subject were the sons of artisans and were aiming at some manual occupation. In a large number of such cases drawing was the only course in the central school which they followed.

The course in ancient languages, says the report, is greatly handicapped because pupils often come up from the primary schools very badly equipped. They are supposed to have acquired the skills of reading, writing and ciphering before entering a central school at the age of twelve; but there is no admission test and

[1] See Duruy, *L'Instruction publique de la Révolution*, chap. v.

the result is that some of the pupils are 'sans savoir écrire ni lire'. The professors, in accordance with the law of 25 October 1795, cannot require any other qualification than that of age and must therefore admit them if this condition be fulfilled. Although this course ought to last two years some teachers give only one year to it, but others carry it on for three or four. Usually eight lessons a *décade* are given and the pupils are arranged if possible in two or three groups and taken at various times. The report states that on the whole teachers of ancient languages are less well qualified than those who take the other courses, and that barely a third of them are able to teach Greek. It emphasises the importance of establishing some link between this course and that of general grammar in the third section.

The course in natural history lasts normally two years and also has eight lessons in the *décade*. The content tends to vary according to the locality. For example, in a neighbourhood like that of Montpellier or Strasbourg where there is a school of medicine the course will most probably stress botany. In a mining area mineralogy and geology will be the chief interests. Next to drawing, mathematics is the most successful course. Here again it normally lasts two years and eight lessons in the *décade* are devoted to it. It includes arithmetic and geometry. Physics and chemistry is almost as popular as mathematics and is normally oriented towards local industries—agriculture, manufactures or arts. In some *écoles centrales* the teaching of these subjects has been handicapped by lack of apparatus, and the Conseil hopes that this deficiency will be rectified.

The course in general grammar which comes in the third section (pupils over sixteen) is fortunate in having attracted some of the best-qualified teachers. In some

places it is well patronised, but it tends to be handicapped by lack of adequate preliminary preparation
on the part of the pupils. Often it proves necessary to
confine the course to a study of French grammar,
though some introduction to logic may be included.
Belles lettres is one of the least popular courses and one
of the most difficult to conduct, largely owing to its
lack of connection with the preliminary course in
Classics. By the time the pupil has reached the third
section at the age of sixteen he will have forgotten the
smattering of Latin—and perhaps of Greek—which he
learnt when he was aged twelve to fourteen. History,
again, has proved a difficult course to organise, mainly
because its content and aim have not been sufficiently
defined. Most teachers have divided it into three sections
—ancient history, modern history, and the history of
France. Usually the course has to be covered in two
years, but in some schools it has been possible to
devote three years to it. In any case it attracts few pupils
and some of them will be above school age. Legislation
is another vague subject. The works of Montesquieu,
Hobbes, Beccaria and other political theorists may be
studied, or there may be lessons on French law or
commentaries on the constitution. Here again the
pupils often include more mature students.

The report ends by pointing out that the great weakness of the central schools is the lack of co-ordination
and correlation between the various courses. Each of
them is isolated and unrelated to what has gone before
and what follows. The six-year course of the *collèges*
of the *Ancien Régime* was at any rate progressive and
graduated and had a content which was homogeneous.
For this reason there is a tendency among parents to
send their children, when they leave the primary school,

to private teachers who will provide something on the lines of the old college curriculum. The report also repeats the criticism that the age of twelve is the sole qualification for entry to the central school course and that many children are not ready to begin it. There is therefore need for an intermediate type of school, or a lower division of the central school, which will prepare pupils to follow the programme prescribed by the Daunou law. As a matter of fact, a somewhat similar recommendation had already been put forward in a report made on 27 October 1797 to the Conseil des Cinq-Cents by the scientist Roger-Martin, who was deputy for the Haute-Garonne. He had suggested that the number of *écoles centrales* should be reduced to forty-two, and that in place of those suppressed there should be established intermediate schools forming a link between primary and secondary education. The primary schools would be called *écoles ordinaires* and the intermediate schools *écoles renforcées*.[1] He also proposed that, following on from the central schools, there should be a number of *lycées* which would be institutions of university rank. This scheme was virtually a return to that of Condorcet and it was very keenly debated; but in the end it was turned down and it was decided that each department should keep its central school.

The report of the Conseil d'Instruction Publique also makes the criticism that the number of courses which a pupil can take at the same time should be limited and that there should be tests for entry to a central school and for promotion to courses in the second and third sections. In any case it was obvious that the work generally was too ambitious and more suited to an

[1] See Hippeau, *L'Instruction publique*, ii, 300.

13-2

institution of higher education. There is a recommendation that the length of the holidays should be officially determined and that boarding arrangements should be provided wherever they are necessary. It is reported that complaints have been received from teachers that there is too much interference on the part of the departmental authorities and that salaries in some areas are not regularly paid.

All this certainly exposes the chief weaknesses of the Daunou scheme and of the *écoles centrales* in particular; but at the same time the report expresses the belief that 'the present state of public instruction justifies well-founded hopes and the belief that its usefulness is every day better appreciated by the majority of citizens, and that if a small number of easy improvements were effected the Minister would enjoy the glory of having contributed to its most brilliant progress'. It expresses the opinion that any violent interference with existing schools would be a public calamity. It would merely be necessary to make a few alterations, such as abolishing the rigorous division of the course into three sections and determining admission not on the grounds of age, but rather of aptitude and attainment. It also recommends that there should be an extra chair of ancient languages in every central school and that further chairs in science subjects should be founded where this may prove desirable. Again, it is necessary to have a definite plan of studies; the present system is too vague and unco-ordinated and even the teachers themselves tend not to give the pupils what they really need or what is suited to their capabilities.

As a footnote the Council suggests the formation of a special school for the study of moral and political science. Other special schools already exist, but an institution of this kind is necessary especially for training statesmen. It would be for ethics and politics what the École Polytechnique is for physics and mathematics. An alternative would be to add a few more chairs dealing with these subjects to the Collège de France. Another need is for more *pensionnats*, including some for girls. They should be run by private effort, but the government should foster their establishment by any means in its power. For example, if it approved of a *pensionnat* it could send some of its 'State scholars' there as boarders. Select scholars from the departments might be given places in the Prytanée française at Paris.

The *écoles centrales*, after a career of barely six years and in some cases less, were formally suppressed by a law of 1 May 1802. As Francisque Vial says, 'Si elles ont disparu, c'est parce qu'elles avaient le tort d'être révolutionnaires dans une société qui ne l'était plus.'[1] One by one they disappeared and were replaced by the Napoleonic *lycées* which in some ways harked back to the colleges of the *Ancien Régime*. It is a little difficult to form a comprehensive judgement as to their effectiveness because they differed so much one from another. For example, at Besançon the central school had over 500 pupils, while that at Châteauroux soon collapsed entirely owing to lack of support. For reasons like this the opinions of educational historians as to the value and importance of these schools are varied. Vial asserts that we have little direct knowledge of what the *écoles centrales* actually *did*, and that the contemporary reports about them tend to be biased. This judgement may be open to question. As has been shown, there are contemporary statistics available and a great many studies

[1] *Trois siècles de l'histoire de l'enseignement secondaire* (Paris, 1936), p. 161.

of individual central schools, based on local research, have been carried out.[1] Reports again, such as that of 1800, to which reference has been made, are quite ready to criticise existing defects and to suggest remedies. It seems fair to say that, even if the central schools were only a qualified success they do present some interesting features. They were an almost complete antithesis to the colleges of the *Ancien Régime* in their organisation (or lack of it), their curriculum (which was practical and utilitarian rather than 'cultural'), and their aim (which was to produce republican citizens and not ecclesiastics, lawyers and scholars). They were more like technical schools than the academic *collèges*. But the widening of the curriculum and the stress laid on scientific, experimental and practical subjects were destined in the long run and in spite of set-backs to have far-reaching results. It was realised that the function of higher education is to extend and propagate knowledge, and not merely to rely on tradition; and this belief had been common to all Revolutionary educationists alike, however much they differed in matters of detail.

[1] A list of some of these will be found in the Bibliographical Appendix, below, p. 258.

14 The Consulate. The Chaptal report of 1800. The Fourcroy law of 1802

The Directory came to an end in 1799. It had proved unsuccessful both in managing home affairs and in carrying on war against foreign powers. The Council of Five Hundred was dissolved, and under a new constitution Napoleon became First Consul, with two colleagues. An elaborate system of government comprising a Senate, a Tribunate, a Corps Législatif and a Conseil d'État was established; but the real authority and legislative initiative lay in the hands of the First Consul. In the departments administrative power was entrusted to officials called prefects who were appointed by the First Consul and were responsible directly to the Minister of the Interior; they were rather like the *intendants* of the *Ancien Régime*. Every *arrondissement* had its sub-prefect and every municipality its mayor. Thus the whole system was unified and in effect centralised.

The Daunou law of 25 October 1795 remained in force until 30 April 1802, so that the Consulate did not take any hasty action with regard to national education. It did, however, institute inquiries into the existing state of affairs, so that when legislation was ultimately enacted it was at any rate based on some knowledge of the situation. The way was paved by a report[1] dated 9 November 1800 and made to the Council of State (which had the right to initiate laws) by Jean-Antoine Chaptal who was Minister of the Interior. It begins with a rather sketchy account of the development of

[1] Published in *Moniteur*, An IX, no. 19.

public instruction in France and it commends the projects of Condorcet and Talleyrand; but it stresses the ineffectiveness of the Convention's educational activities. 'Instruction today is as the Convention left it—a few primary schools in the towns and practically none in the country areas; one central school in each department; several efficient special schools—e.g. those of medicine, music and civil engineering...But practically everywhere the central schools are deserted and if one wants to discover the cause of the lack of success of this new kind of institution, one can find it in the defects of its organisation. Perhaps I need merely compare the old type of education with the new in order to demonstrate this truth.' Chaptal goes on to commend the *Ancien Régime* for having secured well-qualified teachers, whether in colleges or among the members of teaching congregations. He praises the gradation of the curriculum in the colleges and their organisation and sense of community. But he acknowledges that they were too much hampered by tradition and that they gave the pupil too little encouragement to think for himself. In short, one can regard it as a fundamental fact that under the *Ancien Régime* public instruction certainly needed reforming, but it is undeniable that its teaching methods were admirable. Compared with it, 'the system of instruction which exists today is essentially bad, not so much owing to the nature of the instruction itself, but owing to faulty organisation'.

Chaptal repeats the criticisms which had so often been made already. In many places primary schools are lacking, and a generation now approaching its twentieth year is growing up in absolute ignorance. 'In a representative government instruction is everywhere essential. All citizens are called upon to vote for the election of magistrates; and anyone who cannot read or write is at the mercy of those who possess these arts. Reading, writing, arithmetic and elementary ideas as to the social contract—this is the general education which the government owes to all alike. It is an absolute necessity for everyone and for that reason it is a public debt which society has the duty of discharging.' In any case this primary and fundamental education is essential if pupils are to gain any benefit whatever from the subsequent stages of instruction. But the present central schools lack gradation of studies, and they have no definite time-tables or properly organised and co-ordinated courses; and in many cases their staffing is inadequate or incompetent.

In view of these defects Chaptal puts forward the following proposals: Primary education should be provided by the State for children from the age of six to about twelve; and their schools will be entitled *écoles municipales*. There should be at least one of these in every commune and it will normally have about 250 pupils. In order to secure the co-operation and interest of the home, teachers will be nominated by fathers of families and the final appointments made by the sub-prefects. The cost of the teachers' salaries will be met half by the municipality and half by the *arrondissement*. In these municipal schools the curriculum will include the three 'R's' together with elementary surveying. Next above them come *écoles communales*, one of which will normally be situated in the chief town of each *arrondissement*—it would have been more appropriate to call them *écoles d'arrondissement*. No pupil will be admitted below the age of ten and the course will last four or five years. Wherever necessary a *pensionnat* will be provided. The curriculum will embrace French,

Latin, natural history, geography, mathematics, physics and drawing. Modern language courses can also be arranged. Advancement from one stage to the next will be regulated by examination tests. In these schools half the teacher's salary will be contributed by the *arrondissement* and half by the department.

From the communal schools pupils will either go straight out to earn a living or else will proceed to one of the special schools in Paris or elsewhere for a professional training. Chaptal would retain, and if necessary extend and supplement the existing institutions of higher education—e.g. the three medical schools, the Conservatoire des Arts et Métiers, the Museum and the Collège de France, together with the Institute which should have a permanent secretary for each of its three classes. The cost of the whole scheme of public instruction is estimated at 9,572,600 francs; but independent schools are to be allowed in order to supplement the State provision of education. 'The government has the right to demand that no one shall exercise the profession of teacher unless he is a French citizen, unless he has taken an oath of fidelity to the constitution, and unless he has informed the local authority that he is opening a school. But once that has been done it is merely necessary to exercise official supervision. The actual nature of the instruction given is the business of the teacher...To restrict the instruction to prescribed methods, to circumscribe it within limits laid down by the government, would be to deprive it of its finest characteristic—independence.' One can hardly be surprised that this recommendation did not commend itself to the First Consul and that Chaptal's report was not accepted.

Four months later, however, by a questionnaire

dated 16 March 1801 an inquiry was made into the state of national education.[1] It was sent out to prefects and it is possible that in some cases the replies were affected by personal or local feeling; but taken as a whole there seems no reason to believe that they are not reliable. The overall picture is anything but a satisfactory one. To take some typical examples: Loire-Inférieure complains that there are no primary schools whatever in the rural communes. Vendée and Hérault comment on the incapacity and lack of a sense of vocation on the part of *instituteurs*. In Vaucluse and Ille-et-Vilaine public instruction is 'practically non-existent'. Other departments complain of the indiscipline and delinquency of the children. In Pas-de-Calais 'young people are given over to the the most abject ignorance and the most alarming vagrancy'. Their manners are 'farouches et barbares'. From many quarters comes the demand for a return to regular religious training and to a re-establishment of the primary schools run by the Christian Brothers or by teaching congregations of women such as the Ursulines or Sisters of Charity. Such private schools as have been revived 'are much more frequented than the State schools; religious instruction is given in them'. In this connection it should be noted that some important work, especially in the much-neglected field of primary education, was actually being developed by private effort; and it was this that many of the prefects' reports wished to encourage. The Concordat between the Pope and Napoleon, which was signed on 15 July 1801, put an end to the schism which had been created by the Civil Constitution of the Clergy and made Catholicism

[1] See A. Aulard (ed.), *Statistiques des préfets en l'an IX et l'an X* (Paris, 1897).

once more the State religion. This opened the doors to the congregations which had been suppressed or exiled in 1792; and they were now free to return and reinforce the efforts of the private teachers who had been doing something to fill up the deficiencies in the existing situation. The Christian Brothers, who had emigrated to Italy and elsewhere, or who had been living in France as ordinary civilians, were authorised by a Consular decree of 3 December 1803 to resume their work as an organised Institute. The Ursulines, who had been outstanding teachers of girls in both primary and secondary schools under the *Ancien Régime*, also started work again. Both these teaching congregations were approved by Napoleon and were incorporated in the national system of education which he set up by a series of decrees between 1806 and 1811.

It was on the basis of the prefects' replies to the inquiry of March 1801 that Fourcroy, who was a member of the Conseil d'État and had taken an active part in this investigation, drew up a new project.[1] This was presented to the Legislative Corps on 19 April 1802. Once again the school system is divided into three stages—primary schools established by the communes, secondary schools which may be supplied either by the communes or by private initiative, and *lycées* which will replace the central schools. Above them will come the special professional schools. The teachers in the primary schools will be appointed by local mayors and municipal councillors. The commune will provide housing accommodation, but the salary will depend on fees paid by the parents and determined by the local authority. Not more than one-fifth of the pupils are to be exempted from payment of fees on grounds of

[1] See Hippeau, *L'Instruction publique*, I, 487–519.

poverty. The ultimate responsibility for primary schools rests with the sub-prefects who must inspect them once a month and send a report on them to the prefect. In the secondary schools the curriculum will be similar to that proposed by Chaptal for his *écoles communales*. Latin has its place but not a dominating one, and emphasis is given to French, mathematics, geography and history. The government will encourage the establishment of secondary schools by admitting their most successful pupils to free places in the *lycées* and by giving bonuses to the teachers who have the largest number of pupils qualifying for such awards. Secondary schools, whether established by a local authority or by private initiative, must first obtain government sanction, and in both cases are subject to supervision and inspection by prefects.

Above the secondary schools the 1802 project provides for thirty *lycées* maintained at State expense. Their course will last for six years and they will carry to a higher degree the subjects started in the secondary school. The curriculum will include ancient and modern languages and literature, the sciences, and in short 'everything which pertains to a liberal education'. But *lycées* need not all be of exactly the same type. The curriculum will be a progressive one, but should to some extent be determined by local conditions and needs. There should be at least eight teachers in each *lycée*, and in addition three responsible masters whose offices can be paralleled in the French *lycée* of the present day—a *proviseur* or head-master who is ultimately responsible for the school, a *censeur*, who is particularly concerned with its academic work and discipline, and a *procureur* or bursar. The government will fix salaries and give bonuses to successful teachers.

A pension scheme is also indicated. The pupils will be in four categories—those admitted by competitive examination from the secondary schools; 'State scholars' appointed directly by the government and of whom 2,400 will be sons of military men or civil servants; boarders; day-boys. In the last two cases fees will be paid by the parents, but the amount of them will be determined by the government and may vary according to local conditions. There will be a governing body composed of the 'principal magistrates', with the *proviseur* as a member, and they will audit the school accounts and exercise a general supervision. Three inspectors-general, appointed by the First Consul, will have the duty of visiting the *lycées* and reporting to the government on their success or defects. The professors also will be selected by the First Consul from a list of candidates recommended by a committee of three inspectors and three members of the Institute. All this will ensure 'a good choice of men whose duty it will be to train young people and give them both a sound education and an example of high moral standards'.

Fourcroy's project on April 1802 goes on to deal with higher education in the special professional schools. Those already in existence are to be retained, but ten schools of law should be provided and the number of schools of medicine raised from three to six. The standard of qualification for degrees also in these subjects should be raised. For the sciences four new special schools are needed—in natural history, in physics, in chemistry and in higher mathematics. There should also be more provision for technical education, and a school of political economy associated with geography and history should be established for the training of statesmen and public functionaries. The study of astronomy must be encouraged by securing the appointment of a professor of this subject in all existing observatories, and especially in the principal ports because of its relevance to the art of navigation. To the schools of art in the country an extra one will be added. 'This new school will not compete with those already existing in various towns and especially the school in what used to be Belgium. Far from wishing to destroy these, the government, in order to do justice to the enthusiasm of those citizens who have been maintaining them at their own expense and of the teachers who have been reviving in them the talent of the famous Flemish painters, will neglect no means of increasing their usefulness and encouraging their development.' Music will also be fully catered for; 'we ought not to neglect an art which civilises manners, stimulates courage and affords us so much enjoyment'.

An even more urgent need is for a professional school for the scientific study of agriculture. Hitherto this subject has been neglected because scientists are not normally much interested in farming, and those who do carry on this work usually do it by rule of thumb and traditional methods. A separate section of Fourcroy's report deals with military training—a subject of vital importance in view of the campaigns which France was carrying on in many parts of Europe and in the Near East. The special school which deals with this matter will not be reserved for a particular caste, as was the case under the *Ancien Régime*, but will be open to any pupil from a *lycée* who can pass the tests for admission. Five hundred students of this kind will take a two-year course and will be maintained at public expense. This two years will count as part of the period of conscription (which had been re-introduced in September 1798), and the most successful students will be posted to commissions in the army on leaving the school. The Minister for War will be responsible for this institution and the professors will be appointed directly by the First Consul. In the case of teachers in all the other special schools the procedure will be as follows: two candidates will be put forward for a vacancy, one by the inspectors-general and one by the Institute; but in the case of such schools as are already in existence they may themselves also nominate a third candidate. The government, however, will make the final decision.

The report includes a section in which a hope is expressed that national education may benefit from private benefactions. 'The government, impressed by the troubles which have resulted from the practically total destruction of the former endowments of educational establishments, and realising the need to encourage once again generosity and the love of learning in one of its most attractive and useful forms, is determined to regard such endowments with the deepest and most lasting respect.' The cost of the scheme to the government, however, will be rather less than that estimated in Chaptal's project. It was now reduced to a total of 7,313,000 francs.

The presentation of Fourcroy's proposals was followed by a good deal of discussion and criticism. It was maintained, for example, that the central schools on the whole were getting to work and showing results. It was noted that the report contained no reference to religion. But what strikes the modern critic most forcibly is the emphasis which Fourcroy puts on higher education and the relatively small concern for the primary stages. The *lycées* and the special schools are to be maintained at State expense, but elementary education is left very largely to local initiative, and it is hoped that it will be supplemented by private effort. It is obvious that in a time of total war expenditure on education is bound to be reduced. Doubtless Fourcroy was very conscious of this and was anxious to do his best for technical education which tends to attract most attention under such conditions. But even so the outstanding need and basis to all this educational endeavour was the provision of an efficient and organised system of primary schools. 'The primary school', said the report, 'is the need of all and therefore should be the concern of all'; but if that implied leaving much of it to private initiative, while elaborate arrangements were made for technical and professional education, it would seem that the emphasis was put in the wrong place. However that may be, Fourcroy's project became law on 30 April 1802. It was passed in the Corps Législatif by 251 votes to 27 and it may be regarded as the last act in the educational history of the Revolution. It was a kind of compromise between the fundamental reforms for a complete democratic State system, which earlier revolutionary educationists had put forward, and the reaction to a despotic system which did eventually, in the Napoleonic 'University', provide an organised and highly centralised system of public instruction.

15 Educational influence of the Revolution. Napoleon and the Imperial University

There is some considerable difference of opinion among historians as to the value and significance of educational activity during the Revolution. A. F. Théry, when he arrives at this period, says bluntly 'On n'étudie pas la vide; on n'analyse pas le néant'[1]—though this does not prevent him from devoting twelve pages to the subject. The Abbé Allain, again, asks 'Is it really true that the men of the Revolution had at any rate the honour of discovering and formulating the fruitful ideas which have, so far as education goes, become the common inheritance of enlightened men of all parties—ideas which have inspired governments which have since had the task of rebuilding the ruins?'[2] He gives an emphatic 'No' as an answer to his own question, and claims to have proved from his own researches and from available statistics that these ideas had already been expressed in the *cahiers*, and especially in those submitted by the clergy. He speaks strongly from the point of view of a churchman; but in addition to the *cahiers* one could also emphasise the influence of pre-Revolution *philosophes* and parliamentarians. Gabriel Compayré, on the other hand, praises the educational work of the Revolution. He asks us to forget the activities and proposals of the extremists and to consider the views expressed by more moderate reformers—and especially the claim that it is the right of every citizen to receive as extended an education as

[1] *Histoire de l'éducation en France* (2 vols, Paris, 1858), II, 187.
[2] *L'Œuvre scolaire de la Révolution* (Paris, 1891), pp. 341–2.

he is capable of attaining, and the duty of the State to make this possible. If the statesmen of the Revolution period failed to achieve this, it was not their fault. Conditions made it impossible—foreign and civil wars, lack of funds and general upheaval. Louis-Grimaud, again, regards the Revolution as the 'point of departure of a new era in which the State will have the exclusive right of instruction'.[1]

There is some truth in the statement that from an educational point of view the work of the French Revolution can be summed up in the two words 'destruction' and 'projects'; but it is not the whole truth. It may be conceded that the practical achievement of the Revolution was, on the whole, mediocre. It did not really succeed in setting up a complete national system of education on the ruins of the institutions of the *Ancien Régime* which it had destroyed, although the central schools were an important experiment. There was one field, as has already been pointed out, in which it had some notable successes—that of higher and professional education. Here its outstanding creation was the Institute. It also preserved the Collège de France and the Bibliothèque Nationale and founded the institutions which were described in chapters 10 and 11. But even if in the days of the Convention France was outstanding in Europe in technical and further education, her pre-eminence declined as the nineteenth century progressed; and in any case this was no efficient substitute for what the Revolution had destroyed. Professor Adamson has the last word when he says 'In the field of concrete achievement the innovators failed badly, but in that of abstract principle their discussions gave currency to certain doctrines which from that

[1] *Histoire de la liberté d'enseignement*, II, 455.

date onwards formed integral parts of French liberalism —laicisation of schools, gratuitous public instruction, obligatory schooling without respect of sex'.[1]

This does not mean that every report or proposal put up in the revolutionary assemblies included all these principles; but taken together they may be expanded as follows: (a) Education is primarily the concern of the State, and even if 'free' (i.e. independent) schools are allowed they must be supervised by State authorities and conform to State requirements. (b) This means that the control of education by the Church is no longer permissible. (c) This State system must be co-ordinated and cover national needs. Primary education at least should be compulsory and the fullest opportunity afforded to all citizens, however poor or humble, and of either sex, to obtain the most complete education of which they are capable. This is indeed a fundamental human 'right'. (d) In order to achieve this the principle of gratuity should be introduced. It may be complete or apply only to certain stages of the national system or in cases of poverty. If there is any form of fee system ample bursaries should be provided. (e) Education as far as possible should be practical and utilitarian and related to the ordinary life of the ordinary citizen. At the same time it should be a means of training the reason, and not merely of imparting information. The traditional curriculum of the *collèges*, therefore, which was based on the Classics, should be replaced by one in which the sciences and mathematics play a conspicuous part. Great stress should also be laid on French both as a subject of study and particularly as a medium of instruction. Room should be found for history and geography and modern languages. (f) The

[1] *A Short History of Education* (London, 1919), p. 239.

educational system should include facilities for research and for extending knowledge. This can be done
by the application of the human understanding alone
without any need of supernatural revelation; and it will
tend to the 'perfecting' of society and its members.
(g) Education should emphasise instruction in the rights
and duties of the citizen, and inculcate intelligent,
informed and responsible loyalty to the established
government. There should, however, be no religious
teaching in State schools.

It may be conceded that in pursuit of these aims it
was not always easy to be consistent, as indeed has been
realised by other régimes in later days. For example,
there was the problem of reconciling individual liberty
with the overall claims of the State. 'Liberty' and
'Equality', as items in the Republican slogan, ultimately
meant that in the eyes of the law all citizens were equal
—i.e. that they enjoyed equality of political status. The
'Rights of Man' applied to all members of the community without distinction. Class privileges, tax exemptions, seignorial dues and all the evidences which
distinguished class from class under the *Ancien Régime*
were swept away; but that did not mean that the State
abrogated any control—and not least in a national
system of education. On the contrary, so far as educational establishments were concerned, they were
strictly supervised, even if and when they were allowed
to be otherwise independent. Specially prepared text-
books and regular inspection ensured that the doctrines
of State supremacy and republican 'morality' were
being taught. Observance of the *décadi* and participa-
tion in national festivals were enforced. Condorcet was
indeed the only revolutionary statesman of any note
who asserted that no public body should have authority

to prevent the teaching of theories contrary to its own political views. He proclaimed religious toleration and would allow independent schools; and he opposed the use of the school as a means of spreading nationalist propaganda. The 'Rights of Man' was to be explained and based on reason, and not taught as a dogma. But Talleyrand had no hesitation in advocating that children of tender age in the primary school should be indoctrinated with the principles of the Constitution of 1791. 'The declaration of the Rights of Man and the principles of the constitution', he asserts, 'will form in future a new catechism for childhood and will be taught even in the most elementary schools throughout the kingdom.'[1] This was an attitude which became more and more common as the Revolution developed, and it is seen in its most acute form in Lepelletier's scheme for conditioning children in State boarding schools.

Perhaps it is only fair, however, to bear in mind the political conditions of the time. If an entirely new régime, based in theory upon liberty and equality, were to be made effective, it was important that the ordinary rank and file of the French people should be led to understand what the change really meant—its rights and its responsibilities; and the most easy and obvious way of doing this was by means of a national system of popular education. But the difficulty of reconciling individual freedom of thought and action with nationalist requirements prescribed by the State is one which remains and which sometimes confronts even modern democracies. For example, the United States, which claims to be the Land of Liberty and prints 'Liberty for all' on its postage-stamps, proscribes the teaching of religion in State schools but requires children to salute

[1] See Hippeau, *L'Instruction publique*, I, 46.

the flag and take an oath of allegiance to the State—and that without any 'Cowper-Temple' clause which would permit of their withdrawal from this performance if the parents had conscientious objections to it. But the practice, rather like the use of the school for propaganda during the French Revolution, has obviously grown out of the basic need to inculcate loyalty to a new régime among the children of immigrants who are to be future citizens.

Of course, under the *Ancien Régime*, when educational establishments of all kinds were ultimately under the control of the Church, schools had been used for propaganda purposes. Their aim was not to encourage and develop independent thought on religious or political issues, but to inculcate Catholicism which was the official State religion. In order to combat heresy an attempt was made, as has been seen,[1] in 1698 to ensure that children went to Catholic schools and were there instructed in the 'mysteries of the Catholic religion'. But in the background there was a strong political motive based on the fear that the growth of Protestantism might result in a Huguenot *imperium in imperio* which might destroy national unity and undermine the authority of the Crown. But when the old order of things was swept away and the supremacy of the Church and royalty alike was overthrown the school became an important instrument for inculcating and explaining, not the old religion, but the new political doctrines. So among the things that the Revolution did was to bring to the fore the idea that one of the main purposes of the school is to serve the State and educate youth in the virtues of nationalism; and that is an idea which has tended to develop and expand in Europe and elsewhere

[1] See above, p. 1.

ever since. But as Robert Ulich says, 'A policy of education based exclusively on the idea of patriotism and utility was bound to destroy the very premiss of a liberal education—freedom to think without concern for immediate practical results.'[1]

The Directory had left unresolved the possible conflict between individual and State rights in education. The revival of independent schools and the return of the teaching congregations, however, had tended to foster an anti-republican spirit and this provoked a reaction on the part of the State. By the law of 5 February 1798 it had tried to keep such schools under close supervision; but when the Napoleonic régime was established the principle of State control was carried a good deal further. France was now given a new legal code and a strong and highly organised, bureaucratic administration, which included a State system of education. The 'equality', which had swept away the class privileges of the *Ancien Régime* and which made all citizens equal in the sight of the law, was certainly preserved; but the new government put all real authority and legislative initiative into the hands of the First Consul, so that the centralised absolutism of the *Ancien Régime* was reproduced and even emphasised, and in its rather different way the rule of Napoleon was as complete and autocratic as that of Louis XIV, as well as being administratively more efficient. As might be expected, national education was profoundly affected by such a situation. Napoleon himself in 1806 wrote: 'There cannot be a firmly established political state unless there is a teaching body with definitely recognised principles.'[2] What those principles were

[1] *The Education of Nations* (New York, 1961), p. 151.
[2] See A. Delfau, *Napoléon et l'instruction publique* (Paris, 1902), p. 16.

216

found expression in the institution and organisation of the Imperial University which was founded by the laws of 10 May 1806 and 17 March 1808. The title 'University' was applied to a teaching corporation embracing all kinds and all levels of education and entirely dependent on the State. This corporation had the monopoly of national education. 'There shall be constituted, under the title of "Imperial University", a body charged exclusively with instruction and public education throughout the Empire.' In the law of 1808 this enactment is developed in detail. 'No school, no educational institution of any kind whatsoever, shall be permitted to be established outside the Imperial University, without the authorisation of its chief. No one may open a school or teach publicly without being a member of the Imperial University and a graduate of one of its faculties.' Thus the whole school system was centralised and organised under governmental control. The official at the head of its administration was entitled 'Grand Master', and he was assisted by a Conseil de l'Université. The University itself was divided into thirty-four regional 'académies', each presided over by a 'rector'.

The Napoleonic system did not, however, like many Revolutionary projects, exclude religious teaching; on the contrary, it used this as yet another means of strengthening the political régime. Reconciliation with the Catholic Church had been effected by the Concordat of 1802, but that did not mean that the Church recovered its control of national education. The *petits séminaires*, depending on archbishops and bishops, were, it is true, allowed to arrange their own curricula and appoint their own teachers; but otherwise, in virtue of a decree of 9 April 1809, they had to conform to regulations laid down by the Grand Master of the University. All private schools also had to pay a special tax (*retribution universitaire*).[1] The purpose of the national educational system under Napoleon is clearly defined as follows: 'All schools of the Imperial University will take as the basis of their instruction (i) the teaching of the Catholic religion, (ii) fidelity to the Emperor, to the imperial monarchy which is entrusted with the happiness of the people, and to the Napoleonic dynasty which ensures the unity of France and all the liberal ideas proclaimed in the constitution; (iii) obedience to the regulations of the teaching body, the object of which is to secure uniformity of instruction and to train for the State citizens who are attached to their religion, their prince, their country and their family.'

Thus, just as surely as in some of the more extreme proposals set forth during the Revolution, the educational system was organised to subserve the State and to be an agent of propaganda for the government, which in this case meant the autocratic rule of Napoleon. Moreover, the Grand Master of the University, on admission to his office, was required to take the following oath to the Emperor: 'Sire, I swear to Your Majesty before God to fulfil all the duties which are imposed upon me; not to use the authority vested in me for any other purpose than the development of citizens attached to their religion, their prince, their country and their parents; to further by all means in my power the progress of enlightenment, sound learning and good morals, to perpetuate all traditions to the glory of your dynasty, the happiness of children and the

[1] For details see A. Aulard, *Napoléon et le monopole universitaire* (Paris, 1911), pp. 178–80.

peace of parents.' Again, members of the Imperial University were required to 'contract civil obligations under oath which will bind them to the teaching corporation. They will promise obedience to the Grand Master in every duty which he may lay upon them in our service and for the benefit of instruction. They will undertake not to leave the teaching corporation and their duties in it without obtaining permission from the Grand Master'. The administration of the Imperial University and its constituent institutions was elaborately organised with a hierarchy of officials, as well as of teachers. It was in fact a kind of laicised Society of Jesus.

As far as the actual schools were concerned, primary education received the least attention. The Grand Master was instructed to encourage and to license the Brothers of the Christian Schools and other teaching congregations, though they were of course liable to supervision by the University. Bishops were also asked to do their utmost to recruit lay teachers for elementary schools where it was not possible to secure the services of Christian Brothers. Napoleon, however, was more interested in secondary education which would appeal especially to the *bourgeoisie*. This social group had become important during the Directory and Napoleon wished to secure its support. The existing central schools were abolished and a different system of secondary education was substituted. This was given in several different types of institution. In the first place there were thirty *lycées* which were mainly boarding-schools and were supported by the State. In them Classics and mathematics were the staple of a course which lasted six years. Next came the *collèges* which were (and still are) municipal or communal secondary schools of a somewhat lower grade than the *lycées*. In them the curriculum included French, Latin, the elements of geography and history and mathematics. There were also independent schools called *instituts*, which were of equal rank with the *collèges*, and in addition boarding-schools which might send their pupils to attend courses in a *lycée* or *collège*. Fees were paid, but the State provided 6,400 scholarships of which 2,400 were ear-marked for the sons of military officers or civil servants. Seminaries flourished because tuition in them was free and they were not necessarily confined to candidates who would proceed to the higher type of theological college (*grand séminaire*) which prepared for holy orders.[1] But all schools alike were included in the University and were amenable to its regulations. Thus in essence it comprised four types of teaching institution—primary schools, secondary schools, university faculties and establishments of higher education. As regards these last two groups, ten faculties of theology and thirteen each of law and of medicine, situated in various French cities, were included in the Imperial University. To these were added two new types of faculty—those of Science and Arts; there were fifteen of the former and twenty-seven of the latter. They continued and amplified the course given in the *lycées* and were not professional or vocational. Thus the *lycées* led on to them or to the special schools such as the École Militaire or the École Normale Supérieure. This latter institution had been founded in 1808. Its students were selected by the inspectors-general of the University from all parts of France, and they followed courses in the École Poly-

[1] A decree of 1811 sought to close *petits séminaires* in towns where there was a *lycée*; but it was not very effective.

technique and Museum as well as in their own college. At the end of their two-year course they were posted by the Grand Master to some suitable vacancy in one of the University establishments.

It has been suggested that Napoleon modelled his Imperial University on a scheme which had already been put into practice in the University of Turin; but although, as has been said, it has something in common with the Society of Jesus, it is obviously in many ways reminiscent of projects put forward during the Revolution itself. It reminds one, for example, of Turgot's scheme for a Council of National Education which was to have the direction of all kinds of educational institution throughout the country; or again of the system advocated by Rolland with his primary schools, *demi-collèges*, *collèges de plein exercice* and universities, and his proviso that if independent schools are allowed they shall be rigorously supervised. Be that as it may, the whole Imperial University seems to have been modelled on military lines, and it has been not inaptly described as a 'civilian army'. The life and organisation of the *lycée*, in particular, illustrate Napoleon's attitude to national education. The school became a copy of the regiment. It was divided into companies, each of twenty-five pupils, with a sergeant and four corporals. The school-life was regulated by drum-signals and in many *lycées* periodic 'route marches', to the accompaniment of military music, were a regular feature of the curriculum. The school uniform of the pupils consisted of a green coat with a light blue collar and trimmings and metal buttons stamped with the name of the *lycée*. Their trousers were blue and the elder boys sported a cocked hat. One of the chief school punishments was to deprive the pupil of his right to wear this costume and to substitute for it 'un habit d'étoffe grossière'. Even the teachers, as members of the University, were required by law to wear a uniform. It comprised a black suit with a palm embroidered in blue silk on the left breast. The headmaster (*proviseur*) was allowed an extra piece of trimming. When on duty teachers had also to wear a black gown together with the coloured *chausse*, *chaperon* or *épitoge* (the French equivalent of the academic hood) on their left shoulder. Thus everything down to the most trivial details was closely regulated and the ultimate aim was obviously not to produce free citizens, but to fit boys to serve the State in the Napoleonic armies or administrative posts, and to stimulate military and patriotic enthusiasm.

16 Subsequent influence in France, England, the United States and Germany

The Grand-Master of the University, Louis-Marcelin de Fontanes, who had been appointed by Napoleon in 1808, continued in office for a short time after the end of the First Empire. The restored King, Louis XVIII, decreed that the University of France should observe the regulations in force until such time as it would be possible to introduce into the existing system of education such modifications as would be adjudged advisable. But Fontanes was a convinced 'clerical', and although he did not go so far as the 'ultras' who demanded the abolition of the University and the resumption of Church control over national education, he did issue a circular in which he asserted that as the throne of St Louis had been restored his religion should more than ever dominate the schools of France—the old doctrine of *Cujus regio ejus religio*. A decree was even obtained which exempted the *petits séminaires* from University control and freed their pupils from the necessity of following courses in *lycées* and *collèges*. In the educational system generally there was an increase in ecclesiastical influence. Bishops were given control of education in their dioceses and members of religious orders were allowed to qualify for teaching simply on the strength of their 'letters of obedience', and without any further University authorisation. From now onwards throughout the middle of the nineteenth century and even afterwards education in France is closely affected by politics, and there is a recurring conflict between the Church and the State as to the control of public instruction. Thus we have the contrasting educational systems of the *Ancien Régime* and the Revolutionary extremists continually in opposition. Against it all stood the ideals of the Enlightenment and of thinkers like Condorcet which opposed despotism in either form, and which sought to give real meaning to the terms 'liberty' and 'equality' and to apply them in the field of education.

After the downfall of Napoleon there had been some revival of the interest which Revolutionary educationists had shown in elementary education. About this time the monitorial system, which had been started in England by Bell and Lancaster, was introduced into France. It was looked upon askance by the Church and the teaching congregations which continued to use the simultaneous method employed by St J.-B. De La Salle; but it was encouraged by the liberals and anti-clericals. So here was another point at issue between the two parties as regards education. A Société pour L'Instruction Élémentaire had been founded as far back as June 1815.[1] It had strong liberal support and favoured the monitorial system. In spite of clerical opposition during the ultra-royalist period of the Restoration it survived and by a royal ordinance of 1831 was recognised as an 'établissement d'utilité publique'. It continued throughout the nineteenth century, with varying fortunes, to oppose 'the encroachments of the teaching congregations and to uphold steadfastly the conviction that secular education supplies the State with the best kind of citizen, and the family with its most enlightened heads'.

In the field of secondary education after the Restoration ecclesiastical influence became more in evidence. The Grand-Mastership of the University was given in

[1] See Buisson, *Dictionnaire de Pédagogie*, II, 2792–6.

1821 to Denis-Luc Frayssinous, who was a Roman Catholic bishop. Religious instruction was made compulsory in the royal colleges, as the *lycées* were now called. Owing to their liberal tendencies Victor Cousin was dismissed from his chair of philosophy in the Faculty of Letters at Paris, and Guizot was also deprived of his professorship of modern history. But after the establishment of the July Monarchy and the accession of Louis-Philippe in 1830 there was an anti-clerical reaction. Cousin and Guizot were restored to their chairs. Teaching congregations, unless specially authorised, were forbidden. Some attempt however was made to reconcile the Church and the University. The Charter of 1830 promised liberty of instruction— i.e. the sanctioning of independent schools. Liberal catholics like Lamennais, Montalembert, and Lacordaire in their journal *L'Avenir*, which with its motto 'Dieu et Liberté' was first published in 1830, demanded that education, like the press, should be 'free'; and they therefore opposed University control. But an important law dating from 1833, which was the work of Guizot as Minister of Public Instruction, made some attempt to reconcile the two tendencies in educational organisation. As in the project put forward by Condorcet in 1792, there were to be three stages in the primary-secondary course—first elementary schools and then higher primary schools leading to the *collèges*. These were to be established by communes, or groups of communes, but religion was not to be excluded from the curriculum. 'The State and the Church are the only effective agents in popular instruction...While the action of the State and the Church is indispensable if popular instruction is to spread and establish itself firmly, it is necessary also that for this instruction to be good and socially useful it should be profoundly religious.'[1] By the 1833 law training colleges were set up in the departments and, in addition to the State schools with their *instituteurs*, the teaching congregations and individuals were allowed to run independent schools, though these were liable to government inspection and their teachers had to be licensed by the civil authorities as well as by the bishops. The lower and higher primary schools were to be supported partly by fees and partly be an education rate levied by the council of the commune and supplemented, if necessary, by a grant from the departmental authority. In accordance with a promise contained in the Charter of 1830 schooling was to be free in these schools for those pupils whose parents could not afford to pay fees; but education was not made compulsory.

The Guizot law, then, was a kind of Concordat between the Church and State, with perhaps a certain advantage to the former. But there was an influential group of thinkers and writers, including such theorists as Saint-Simon and Fourier, who advocated social and political reform and whose doctrines were attracting support among 'progressives'. There were also statesmen who strongly supported the claim of the University to have exclusive supervision of all forms of national education. Thiers, for example, in a report dating from 13 June 1844, asserted that 'the State has the right to will that the child be developed into a citizen filled with the spirit of the constitution, loving its laws, loving our country and having the qualities which will contribute to its greatness and to national prosperity'.[2] Those are

[1] Guizot, *Mémoires* (8 vols, Paris, 1858–67), III, 68.
[2] See R. Niderst, *L'Enseignement primaire en France* (Strasbourg, 1935), p. 41.

words which might well have been spoken in one of the Revolutionary assemblies. Thiers therefore wished to re-establish the control of the State—i.e. the University —over independent educational institutions, and he claimed that the spirit of the Revolution implied that instruction should be given by teachers imbued with loyalty to the established régime.

However, the reactionary Loi Falloux, which dates from 1850, put the power back into the hands of the Church. It abolished the University's monopoly and formed a Counseil supérieur de L'Instruction Publique which included four bishops, and in which the eight University members were in a minority. Training colleges were closely supervised in order to suppress the spread of liberal ideas, and even the press and working-men's associations were strictly regulated. Clergy and members of religious orders were permitted to teach without the University qualification demanded of lay teachers, and primary schools were liable to supervision by local *curés*. Teaching congregations were encouraged and some even of the schools run by public authorities were staffed by them. This was indeed a reversion to something very similar to educational conditions under the *Ancien Régime*. However, the ascendancy of ecclesiastical influence was short-lived. Gustave Rouland, Minister of Public Instruction in 1856, upheld the rights of the State in national education. He did much to encourage lay primary education and to resist the encroachment of the teaching orders. This movement was continued by Victor Duruy who was education minister from 1863 to 1869. He fostered secondary education for girls and widened the course in the *lycées* (which had resumed this title in 1848) and the *collèges*, so as to emphasise mathematics

15-2

and scientific instruction along the lines so often advocated by Revolutionary educationists. He endeavoured to make primary education gratuitous and compulsory, but was unable to get from the Emperor Louis-Napoleon the support necessary to secure this.

Under the Third Republic, however, the influence of the Church once more weakened and the right of the State to control public education was vindicated. Liberal and anti-clerical leaders like Gambetta aimed at building up a strong French nation on the basis of universal popular education. At last, after the lapse of nearly a century, the principles for which the Revolution had stood were realised—to quote Professor Adamson once more, 'Laicisation of schools, gratuitous public instruction, obligatory without respect of sex'.[1] By a law of 1882, initiated by J. F. C. Ferry, the Minister of Public Instruction, the basis of modern French primary education was laid. Schooling was made compulsory from the age of six to thirteen, and all primary education was gratuitous. (The abolition of fees in State secondary schools had to wait until 1930–33). Religious teaching was excluded from State schools, but instead it was enacted that primary education should include 'instruction morale et civique'.[2] Each department was required to provide a training college for primary teachers, and two higher normal schools—one for men and one for women—were established to provide staff for these departmental normal schools. *Lycées* and *collèges* for girls were also founded.

At the beginning of the twentieth century the process of laicisation and State control was carried even

[1] *A Short History of Education* (p. 239).
[2] For details as to its content see E. H. Reisner, *Nationalism and Education* (New York, 1922), pp. 83–91.

further. Although a law of 1886 allowed the formation of *écoles libres* the number of pupils in the State schools had increased greatly, while those in the congregational schools had correspondingly decreased. But a more serious blow was still to come. The revulsion after the Dreyfus affair, in which the clerical party had assumed an anti-semitic attitude, gave rise to a fresh anti-Church campaign. One of its results was the Acts of 1901, 1903, and 1904 which prohibited religious congregations from teaching and closed some 2,250 of their schools. The Separation Act of 1905 ended Napoleon's Concordat with the Pope and relieved the State of the obligation to pay the salaries of clergy; and in 1907 Church property was taken over by the government. There has since been some relaxation of this intransigeant attitude, and today *écoles libres*, run by private individuals or associations, exist and flourish in France. Their teachers, however, are required to hold the qualifications demanded by the Ministry of Public Instruction and they are liable to official supervision. The Third Republic has not inaptly been termed the 'heir of the Revolution';[1] and to this day the whole highly centralised and elaborately organised educational system, adumbrated by Revolutionary theorists like Rolland, Talleyrand and Condorcet, and actually established by Napoleon, is still the main structure of French education, in spite of some modern modifications. It is regarded as a safeguard of national unity and the guardian of French culture.

The western world could never be quite the same after such an upheaval as the French Revolution, and its influence was felt not only in France itself but also

[1] M. Glatigny, *Histoire de l'enseignement en France* (Paris, 1949), p. 104.

in other European countries and in America. The principles for which it stood were at first widely welcomed by those thinkers who found in them a guarantee for the progress and 'perfectibility' of human society, and the inauguration of an era of reason and perpetual peace. They also raised hopes among the under-privileged for political equality and for the abolition of class distinctions and autocratic rule. All these things had their educational implications, but it was the political aspects of the Revolution that interested most sympathisers. In England, for example, the idea that equality before the law implied a system of education sponsored by the State was not generally accepted. The middle and upper classes, as the Revolution progressed, were horrified at the excesses of the mob. They were greatly alarmed at the decree of the Convention (19 November 1792) which offered assistance to any people struggling against its rulers. They deplored the growth of republicanism and deism or atheism, and were inclined to blame the withdrawal of the old restraints and to believe that an extension of popular education might encourage sedition and further licence. Even radicals tended to fear that the institution of a State system might infringe individual rights and afford the government an instrument of political propaganda by means of the school.

It would of course be quite unjustifiable to assert dogmatically that those in this country who, in the period roughly between 1760 and 1830, did advocate a State system were in so doing directly influenced by theories and projects put forward in France before, during, and just after the Revolution. There were other countries—e.g. Prussia—and other educationists —e.g. Pestalozzi—who excited interest. But it is noticeable that, whereas generally speaking the provision of popular education in England—as in France—had for centuries been left to independent initiative (which in most cases meant the efforts of the Church or of private individuals), and had not been regarded as a State concern, at the time of the French Revolution and in the period just following there was a tendency in this country, especially among intellectuals, to question whether or how far this was a desirable state of affairs, and whether or how far the government ought to intervene.

This did not mean, therefore, that such thinkers unanimously and completely accepted the educational programme for which the Revolution stood. The extent to which they did or did not do so can be illustrated by a few typical examples. One of the first in this country to reflect eighteenth-century French influence on educational thought was the economist Adam Smith. He had travelled in France between 1764 and 1766 and had associated with Turgot, Helvétius and other *philosophes*. Like them, he distrusts ecclesiastical control of popular education and therefore sees that the State must assume at any rate some responsibility for it. 'Though the State was to derive no advantage from the instruction of the inferior ranks of the people, it would still deserve its attention that they should not be altogether uninstructed. The State, however, derives no inconsiderable advantage from their instruction... In free countries, when the safety of government depends very much upon the favourable judgement which people may form of its conduct, it must surely be of the highest importance that they should not be disposed to judge rashly or capriciously concerning it.'[1]

[1] *Wealth of Nations*, Bk. V, chap. 1, pt. iii, art. 2.

But Adam Smith does not, like Turgot, advocate a completely State-organised system of education. He proposes the establishment of district schools, maintained partly at public expense and partly by fees, and he suggests that, as a means of encouraging or even enforcing school attendance, an examination test should be required 'before anyone could obtain the freedom in any corporation or be allowed to set up a trade in any village or town corporate'. In secondary and higher education he would rely on voluntary effort because he thinks that endowments tend to discourage effort. Thus Adam Smith is a rather half-hearted exponent of the free and universal State education which was being advocated by some of his French contemporaries; but he paved the way for other thinkers in this country who carried the argument further.

One of them was Thomas Paine, the pamphleteer of the Revolutionary party in England. In his *Rights of Man*, which was described as 'an answer to Mr Burke's attack on the French Revolution',[1] he asserts that 'a nation under a well-regulated government should permit none to remain uninstructed'.[2] Paine was indicted for treason, but he escaped to France and, although an Englishman, was elected in September 1792 to the Convention as deputy for the department of Calais. It seems a fair assumption therefore that he was familiar with the educational projects which were being, or had been, debated in the assembly about this time —for example, those of Condorcet, Lanthenas and Romme. Paine could not speak French and his communications were therefore written out and translated. It was on the motion of Lanthenas that on 17 July 1795 one of the secretaries was instructed to read a speech by

---

[1] Part of the title.   [2] *Rights of Man*, pt. ii, chap. v.

Paine on the Declaration of Rights, and the constitution. Paine had opposed the sentence on Louis XVI, but in his *Rights of Man* he says 'Civil government does not consist in executions, but in making that provision for the instruction of youth and the support of age as to exclude as much as possible profligacy from the one and despair from the other'. So he outlines a scheme for the gratuitous education of six hundred and thirty thousand children, with ample provision for the poor and aged. Parents are to be given an allowance of £4 a year for each child under fourteen years of age in order that he may be sent to school to learn reading, writing and 'common arithmetic.' 'By adopting this method not only the poverty of the parents will be relieved, but the number of the poor will hereafter become less, because their abilities by the aid of education will be greater.' For children whose parents 'though not properly of the class of the poor yet find it difficult to give education to their children' an allowance of ten shillings a year should be made towards their schooling expenses, and two shillings and sixpence for paper and spelling-books. Thus Paine, like the Revolutionary educationists, envisages a scheme of popular instruction, but although it is to be done by State aid, the actual carrying out of the scheme is left to individual effort and not directly to the State itself.

There were others who did not hesitate to go the whole way. Wordsworth, for instance, who was at Cambridge when the Revolution broke out and who spent two long vacations in France, expressed his feelings in the *Prelude*:[1]

> Bliss was it in that dawn to be alive,
> But to be young was very Heaven!

[1] Bk. XI, 108–9.

Even in his more conservative and conventional middle-age he could still advocate the desirability of a national system of education.

> O for the coming of that glorious time
> When, prizing knowledge as her noblest wealth
> And best protection, this imperial Realm,
> While she exacts allegiance, shall admit
> An obligation, on her part, to *teach*
> Them who are born to serve her and obey;
> Binding herself by statute to secure
> For all the children whom her soil maintains
> The rudiments of letters, and inform
> The mind with moral and religious truth.[1]

Among the English writers who accepted and expounded the main principles for which the Revolution stood was the utilitarian philosopher Jeremy Bentham. As we have seen, he had been much influenced by the writings of Helvétius and had been elected as an honorary French citizen in 1792. In his work on penal reform, written ten years later, he said 'In regarding education as an indirect mode of preventing offences, it requires an essential reform. The most neglected class must become the principal object of care. The less parents are able to discharge this duty, the more necessary it is for the government to fulfil it'.[2] His scheme for a 'chrestomathic school' also reproduces the recommendations for curriculum and organisation which the Revolutionary educationists had repeatedly emphasised—the study of subjects which, like mathematics and the physical sciences, are 'conducive to useful knowledge' and are contrasted with the traditional secondary school course which was

[1] *Excursion*, Bk. IX, 293–302.
[2] *Prose Works*, ed. J. Knight (2 vols, London, 1896), II, 51.

common both to England and to the *Ancien Régime* in France.

A more thorough-going English supporter of French Revolutionary ideas on this subject was Mary Wollstonecraft, who was a convinced advocate of State-controlled education. Her belief in 'equality' led her to become an ardent feminist. Like Condorcet and a number of contemporary French women writers[1] she believes that women, no less than men, have a natural 'right' to education; and she sees no reason why boys and girls should not be educated together. But in England and France alike it was many years and by slow stages before her views on female education were implemented. In contrast to Mary Wollstonecraft, her husband, William Godwin, although—as he says—he owes to the French Revolution 'the determination which gave existence' to his *Enquiry concerning Political Justice*, none the less asserts that 'the project of national education ought uniformly to be discouraged on account of its obvious alliance with national government'; and for Godwin 'government even in its best stage is an evil...we should have as little of it as the general peace of human society will permit'.[2] Thus it was possible for the ferment of the French Revolution to work against, as well as for, popular State education.

During the early years of the nineteenth century several attempts were made in the English parliament to translate into actual fact the theories of those who advocated a State system of instruction. In 1806, for example, Samuel Whitbread introduced a bill which, amongst other things, proposed to establish rate-aided

[1] Eg. Mme d'Épinay (1725–83), Mme de Miremont (1735–1811), and Mme de Genlis (1746–1830).
[2] *Op cit*. Bk. III, chap. vii.

parish schools giving two years of free education to those children between the ages of seven and fourteen whose parents could not pay fees. A somewhat similar bill was put forward by Henry Brougham in 1820; and again in 1833 J. A. Roebuck sponsored a thorough-going plan which 'would oblige, by law, every child in Great Britain and Ireland from, perhaps, six years of age to twelve years of age to be a regular attendant at school'. Such instruction might be provided by the State, though the parent would be free to have his child educated in an independent school, if he preferred. Roebuck envisaged a complete scheme including schools of different types and they were to be grouped in administrative areas, the whole being under the control of a cabinet minister.

None of these proposals became law. The only result of Roebuck's action was that in 1833—the year in which the Guizot law was passed in France—the British parliament voted a subsidy for public education. The grant, which became an annual one, was simply paid over to the two societies which had been founded to foster the monitorial schools of Bell associated with the Church of England, and those of Lancaster which were non-sectarian. But these did not mean the estab-lishment of a State system of education. At the back of the opposition to taking this step was the 'religious difficulty' which bedevilled the development of a national system in England throughout the nineteenth century. The conflict was not between clericals and anti-clericals (as in France), because in this country it has been generally accepted that religion, in some form or other, should furnish if not the basis of education, at any rate an ingredient in it. In our case the conflict was between the Church of England and Dissent. As

Adamson points out, 'Education universal, compulsory, gratuitous and secular was the statement of a policy which was gradually developed through discussion under different types of French Revolutionary government. With one exception (if it be an exception) this formula describes the aim in the educational sphere which English Radicals and Liberals strove to attain throughout the nineteenth century. The exception is the principle that public education must be "secular", that is, must not include religious instruction'.[1] The difficulty has been to decide what kind of religious instruction should be included. The schemes put forward by such reformers as Brougham and Roebuck tended to be opposed by the Church of England because it feared that a State system might undermine the monopoly of the national church in national education; and by non-conformists and non-sectarians who opposed that monopoly and distrusted educational institutions which might possibly be used by the State for propaganda purposes and so undermine individual freedom. It was not until 1870, and more completely in 1902, that a compromise was effected and the difficulty gradually resolved.

In the last few decades of the eighteenth century there was a close association between France and the United States. The French had assisted the American colonies to obtain their independence in 1776 and the Declaration of the Rights of Man owes something to the Declaration of Independence. Lafayette was a popular figure in America and Benjamin Franklin in Paris. 'Tom' Paine, although an Englishman, was as much an American as a French citizen, and his writings helped to stimulate the independence movement in the

[1] *English Education*, 1760–1902 (London, 1930), p. 7.

American colonies as they did afterwards to support the revolutionary movement in France. The American Federal Constitution, like the French Declaration of Rights, contained no direct reference to a popular system of education; but in America some important steps had already been taken in this direction. Connecticut, for example, as early as 1650 had introduced a scheme of both primary and secondary education supported by local effort. Massachusetts took a similar step in 1692, and other states followed suit in the eighteenth century;[1] so that French influence at the time of the Revolution tended rather to reinforce than to initiate American effort. In fact, it may well be that the educationists of the Revolutionary assemblies owed more to America than it did to them. C. Hippeau, in the preface to his collection of educational reports and projects put forward during the Revolution, calls attention to the fact that the United States was able to inaugurate schemes of popular gratuitous instruction, for both sexes and at all levels, unencumbered by the ruins of an outworn system and the traditions of a bygone age. 'A people who had never known the fatal dualism which inevitably exists between the State and its citizens, the government and the people, but which governs itself and administers its own affairs, needs only to let itself be guided by the force of its own initiative... If therefore an inhabitant of the United States had been present at the sittings at which Mirabeau, Talleyrand and Condorcet put forward their theories, he could have said—like the Spartan after hearing an eloquent speech by an Athenian citizen

[1] On these early American schemes of popular education see J. E. G. de Montmorency, *State Intervention in English Education* (London, 1902), pp. 135–40.

—"Everything which the orator has put before us we have both the power and the will to carry out."[1]

Be that as it may, as far as education is concerned the statesman Thomas Jefferson provided one of the chief links between the France of the *philosophes* and the Revolution, and the newly-formed republic of the West. Jefferson was in France from 1784 to 1789, and he became Benjamin Franklin's[2] successor as American ambassador to that country. Even the excesses of the Revolution did not weaken his faith in the root principles for which it stood. He espoused the egalitarian teachings of Rousseau and of the Revolution itself, and he applied them to the pioneer conditions of the new Republic. He believed in the 'sovereignty of the people', but he distrusted a centralised government which might mean control by aristocrats or rich landowners. He was consistent therefore in feeling that a scheme of popular education was a matter for each individual state and not for the Federal government itself. In his own State of Virginia he supported a system of free, universal and secular education, with secondary schools for those who could profit by them, and the whole headed and controlled by the College of William and Mary where he himself had been educated. It must have been a progressive institution, for Jefferson had acquired there a good knowledge not only of the Classics and French, but also of mathematics and the sciences.

Jefferson's scheme was not accepted by the legislature of Virginia, largely because of the opposition of religious bodies; but the long-term influence of his

[1] *L'Instruction publique*, I, viii.
[2] On the education influence in France of Benjamin Franklin and of freemasonry see N. Hans, *Comparative Education* (London, 1949), pp. 185–7.

proposals was felt in many American states during the nineteenth century. It remains true to say that his plan had much in common with those put forward by Rolland, Talleyrand and Condorcet. As an article in Monroe's *Cyclopedia of Education*[1] points out, 'Talleyrand's system is practically an exact version in French of Jefferson's scheme of 1779 or his revised scheme of September 1814. The analogy is so close, the plan so foreign to anything hitherto planned in America or England, and Jefferson's French proclivities so clear, that a definitely French influence may be inferred with practical certainty'. As has been indicated, it may in fact be difficult to estimate exactly the debt owed by the one country to the other, but the connection is inescapable. Jefferson was afterwards instrumental in forming a Central College—a name borrowed apparently from the French *école centrale*—which in 1818 became the University of Virginia. To quote again from the *Cyclopedia*,[2] 'In its aim of making worthy citizens, its reliance on State support, its freedom from Church influence, its subordination of the Classics to modern languages, political science and the natural sciences, it reflected the whole current of French educational theory and practice'.

In the case of Germany direct influences of French Revolutionary educational theories are more difficult to trace, though the teachings of the *philosophes*, and particularly of Rousseau and the physiocrats, were well-known to many German intellectuals. Niebuhr, who was born in 1776, says 'Rousseau was the model of most educated people in my boyhood'.[3] Karl von

---

[1] (5 vols, New York, 1911–13), II, 709.

[2] *Ibid.* II, 709–10.

[3] *Geschichte des Zeitalters der Revolution* (2 vols, Hamburg, 1845), I, 83.

Raumer also, in his *Geschichte der Pädagogik*,[1] says 'If Rousseau exercised an incalculable influence in France, if he was the beacon (Pharus) of the revolutionaries, so also in Switzerland and Germany he was the beacon of many educationists'. But just as French language and culture and etiquette had been imitated in the courts of many German princelings ever since the time of Louis XIV, so also the influences of the French Enlightenment and of the physiocrats affected mainly the nobility and ruling classes in Germany. The education of the common people was an indigenous affair and owed little to French influence. As far back as 1717 Frederick William I had made an attempt to establish a system of compulsory elementary education in Prussia. His son, Frederick the Great, who habitually spoke and wrote in French and for a time was a friend of Voltaire, was an enlightened bureaucrat. His accession marked the beginning of the *Aufklärung*— the German version of the Age of Enlightenment. In 1763 Frederick decreed compulsory education for children between the ages of five and thirteen, and he also encouraged teacher-training. Somewhat similar reforms were attempted in Austria during the reign of Maria Theresa, and were due to the Abbot Felbiger.[2]

The development of Neo-Humanism and the study of Greek literature and civilisation, which affected particularly secondary and university education in Germany towards the end of the eighteenth century, were again largely a native development. It was of course not in the least like the adoption of the trimmings of classical republicanism which are a feature of the

[1] 3 vols, Stuttgart, 1843–55, V, 93.
[2] See above, p. 153 n.

241

French Revolution—the fasces and the Phrygian cap of liberty, the crowns of oak-leaves and laurel, the attempts to copy classical institutions and adopt classical terms, as in the case of Lepelletier's *maisons égalité* and the *prytanées* or *lycées*. All this in turn was very different from the classicism of Racine and Corneille and Boileau, though it must be remembered that the majority of the Revolutionary statesmen, like them, had been brought up on the traditional Greek and Latin curriculum of the *collèges* of the *Ancien Régime*, and they tended to look back to an idealised republican society of classical times.

As far as national education is concerned it is interesting to note that Baron von Zedlitz, who was largely responsible for the development of Neo-Humanism in Prussia, was also the inaugurator of a school law of 1787 which introduced a scheme closely resembling those which were about this time being projected in the French Revolutionary assemblies. There was to be a national system with three types of educational institution—rural elementary schools, town secondary schools, and *Gymnasien* giving a higher instruction. Teachers were to become civil servants. The *Abiturientenexamen*, controlling entrance to universities for students leaving the *Gymnasium*, was very similar to the *baccalauréat* established later by Napoleon, though that had primarily the more practical aim of qualifying for civil service posts. Thus the general educational tendency of the Germany of the later eighteenth century lay in the extension of the State system, the increase of State control (though the clergy were sometimes left to function under State supervision), the development of science and modern philosophy in the *Gymnasien* and especially in the universities,[1] and the spreading downwards of educational facilities to the middle and lower classes. With all that went a growth of nationalism. Thus the whole movement has considerable resemblance to the contemporary social and political situation in France, though the ultimate course of events there was very different. Yet the Revolution itself was acclaimed by many of the leading intellectuals in Germany. Poets like Klopstock and Wieland, philosophers like Kant and Hegel and Fichte, statesmen like Wilhelm von Humboldt, all welcomed its advent, even if some of them subsequently had to change their views.

In the field of social and educational regeneration there was another powerful influence at work, especially in Germany and Switzerland—that of Pestalozzi. He spoke and wrote in German, and—as his name indicates —he was of Italian descent; but according to Gabriel Compayré he 'sided with France and the Revolution and at this period he was at heart a Frenchman'.[2] He had certainly been impressed by the teachings of Rousseau and the physiocrats, and had also written an *Essai sur les causes de la Révolution française*,[3] in which he condemns despotism and praises the efforts of those who are seeking to secure the liberty and rights of the people. He appeals to the princes of Germany to give expression to this in their own states. Perhaps this was an acknowledgement of the honorary citizenship of the

[1] In Germany this development of scientific study and research was largely associated with the universities; but in other countries it tended to be carried on in institutions of higher education outside the universities, like the *écoles spéciales* in France.
[2] *Pestalozzi and Elementary Education* (trans Jago, London, 1903), p. 34.
[3] It was not actually printed until 1872. For the educational influence of the French Revolution in Switzerland see J. Godechot, *La Grande Nation* (2 vols, Paris, 1956), II, 652-4.

French Republic which had been conferred on him in 1792;[1] but at any rate it illustrates his interest in the principles for which it stood. As far as Pestalozzi's educational views went, both their theoretical exposition and their practical application spread widely. Among those who were affected by them was Fichte, who became a firm friend of Pestalozzi and who, in his *Addresses to the German Nation*, delivered in 1807–8 after his country's defeat at Jena, urged a re-organisation of the German school system on Pestalozzian lines. Wilhelm von Humboldt, who in 1808 became Director of Public Instruction in Prussia, was also a strong believer in Pestalozzi's teachings, as well as in Neo-Humanism. The activities of these two men were largely responsible for the revival of popular education in Prussia and for the recovery of this country after the downfall of Napoleon.

The period, then, embracing the latter part of the eighteenth century and the early years of the nineteenth marks a kind of watershed in the history of European education. Although full credit must be given to the work of such pioneers as Comenius in the seventeenth century and Basedow in the eighteenth, it remains true that in a sense modern education begins at this epoch. It marks the general acceptance of the principle that popular education should be controlled by the State and not by the Church, and that the State is responsible at any rate for elementary education; the abandonment of the purely classical curriculum of the grammar school and the emphasis on science and 'modern' subjects; the encouragement of free inquiry and research at the university level; and the great

[1] See R. de Guimps, *Life of Pestalozzi* (trans. J. Russell, London, 1890), pp. 96–7 and 104–5.

development of technological instruction which was becoming of increasing importance owing to the expansion of industry.

Of course it is not claimed that the educationists of the Enlightenment and the French Revolution were solely responsible for all this; but every important cultural, political or religious revival has its educational implications, though it is not always easy to isolate them and estimate their real significance and extent. But, as Professor John Roach reminds us, French political and educational ideas were carried all over Europe by means of the press which at this period was becoming everywhere a most important medium for the expression of public opinion.[1] Professor J. W. Adamson also points out that by the beginning of the nineteenth century not only France, but also Prussia and other German states, Switzerland, Holland and Denmark had all accepted the principle that the State was responsible for primary education. That principle was not always firmly established, and from time to time it encountered opposition, for the Church did not give up its educational hegemony without a struggle. In the case of the French Revolution also the sudden acquisition of political liberty, and its concomitant responsibilities, by the 'sovereign people' had brought in its train faction and civil strife, and could even lead to narrow nationalism and eventually to dictatorship. We have seen, and still see, this process at work in various parts of the world. One of the chief handicaps of the French Revolution was that it had to do everything in a hurry

[1] See *New Cambridge Modern History*, IX, chap. vii. In the *Dictionnaire de la Révolution française* (pp. 367–71) there is a list of 243 journals published in France during the Revolution period, but it says that the total was about 1350.

and in an atmosphere of war and confusion. It was hampered by the conflict of political parties and the resistance of those who clung to the old traditions. It could improvise armies and armaments, and wage successful campaigns on several fronts at once; but educational reforms cannot be implemented in the same way or at the same rate; and in this respect therefore it is the long-term influence of the Revolution which is really significant. Countries less liable than France to political upheavals have tended to keep their old educational institutions and develop them gradually. But the effect of the Revolution was to set the whole idea of education in a new direction. In spite, therefore, of the danger of a *post hoc ergo propter hoc* argument, and while giving all due recognition to the work of educationists and educational legislators in other European countries, we still have justification for asserting that modern education, in its administration, its curriculum and its philosophical theory, dates in large measure from the France of the eighteenth century and receives its clearest and most complete exposition at the time of the Revolution.

A summary of Revolutionary educational projects and laws

Rolland (1768)	Mirabeau (1791)	Talleyrand (1791)	Condorcet (1792)	Lepelletier (1793)	Daunou (1795)	Chaptal (1800)
			PRIMARY			
Village schools	Parish schools (supported by dept., but teacher may also receive fees)	One school in every canton (no fees)	One school to every 400 inhabitants (6–10)	State boarding schools: boys 5–12 girls 5–11	One school in every canton (fees payable)	One *école municipale* in every commune (6–10)
			SECONDARY			
(1) *Demi-colleges*; (2) *Colleges* (Fac. of Arts)	*Colleges* (10–about 16)	One school in every district	(i) Secondary (i.e. higher primary schools) (10–13); (ii) Institutes (13–16) (100 of these in France)	(i) Secondary schools (12–16); (ii) Institutes (16–21)	Central schools (12–16+), at least one in every dept.	One *école communale* in every *arrondissement*
			HIGHER			
Universities (higher facs.) A normal school	National *Lycée* in Paris	One institute in every department	(i) *Lycées* university level (nine of these); (ii) National Society of Sciences and Arts	*Lycées* (21–25)	National Institute of the Sciences and Arts; Higher professional schools	Professional schools
			ADMINISTRATION			
Whole system under a *Bureau de Correspondence*	*All* schools to be under control of public authorities, but independent schools allowed	Legislature acting through commissioners appointed by King. Independent schools allowed	Administered by an educational hierarchy. No fees at any stage	Complete State control	State-sponsored system, but independent schools allowed	Financed by State, but independent schools allowed

Chronological Appendix

Educational writings, projects and laws	Other events
1754	
Condillac, *Traité des sensations*	
1751–72	
Encyclopédie	
1758	
Helvétius, *De l'esprit*	
1760	
Agrégation instituted	
1761	
La Chalotais, *Compte rendu*	
1762	**1762**
Rousseau, *Émile* and *Contrat social*	Suppression of Society of Jesus
1763	
La Chalotais, *Essai*	
1767–73	
Condillac, *Cours d'études*	
1768	
Rolland's report	
1772	
Rousseau, *Gouvernement de Pologne*	
Helvétius, *De l'homme*	
1774	**1774**
	Accession of Louis XVI
1775–81	**1775–81**
	American War of Independence
1775	
Turgot, *Memorial to the King*	

Educational writings, projects and laws	Other events
1783	
Philipon de La Madelaine, *De l'éducation du people*	
1784	**1789**
Philipon de la Madelaine, *De l'éducation des collèges*	(May) Meeting of States-General
	(June) Constituent Assembly formed
	(August) *Rights of Man*
	(August) Abolition of *dîmes*
	(November) Nationalisation of Church property
1790	**1790**
	(June) Abolition of nobility
	(July) Civil Constitution of Clergy
1791	**1791**
Mirabeau's project	(February) Abolition of *octrois*
Talleyrand's report	(June) Flight to Varennes
	(August) Declaration of Pilnitz
	(October) Legislative Assembly formed
1792	**1792**
Condorcet's project	(April) Declaration of War on Austria
Lanthenas' project	(August) Abolition of religious orders
Romme's project	(August) Attack on Tuileries
	September massacres
	(September) Convention formed
	(December) Trial of Louis XVI
1793	**1793**
Sieyès-Daunou-Lakanal report	(January) Execution of Louis XVI
Museum (Jardin des Plantes)	(February) Declaration of War on England and Holland
Lepelletier's scheme	(March) Revolt in La Vendée
Paris deputation	(June) Fall of Girondins

Educational writings, projects and laws	Other events
1793 (*cont.*)	1793 (*cont.*)
Romme's report	(July) Great Comm. of Public
Loi Bouquier	Safety formed
Collège de France confirmed	(August) *Levée en masse*
	(November) Fête of Reason
1793–4	1793–4
	Reign of Terror
1794	1794
École des Armes	(May) Cult of Supreme Being
Conservatoire des Arts et Métiers	inaugurated
École de Mars	(July) Execution of Robespierre
Écoles de Santé	(July) Committee of Public
École Polytechnique	Safety reconstructed
Mme Campan's school at	
Saint-Germain	
1795	1795
École Normale	(February) Liberty of worship
École des Langues Orientales	decreed
Bureau des Longitudes	(November) Directory established
Conservatoire de Musique	
École des Beaux Arts	
Daunou law	
	1796
	Bonaparte's campaigns
1797	
Roger-Martin's proposal on	
central schools	
1798	
Decree on independent schools	

Educational writings projects and laws	Other events
1799	1799 ff. (November) *Coup d'état* of 18 Brumaire (December) Consulate established
1800 Chaptal's report	
1801 Prefects' inquiry instituted	1801 (July) Concordat
1802 Fourcroy's law Central schools suppressed	
1804	1804 Napoleon becomes Emperor
1808 Imperial University founded	

Bibliographical Appendix

As was pointed out in Chapters 2 and 3 of this book, in order to understand the educational ideas of the Revolutionaries it is necessary to go back a little and to consider the political, philosophical and social doctrines which were beginning to be enunciated as the *Ancien Régime* was running down to its close. One need hardly refer to Rousseau's *Émile* of which many editions are available and upon which many commentaries have been written; but one should also note his other relevant works such as the *Nouvelle Héloïse* and the *Contrat social*—to say nothing of the *Confessions*. *Émile* should be supplemented by W. Boyd, *The Minor Educational Writings of Jean-Jacques Rousseau* (London, 1910; reprinted by Teachers College, Columbia, 1962). An excellent treatise on Rousseau's life and work and ideas is J. Guéhenno, *Jean-Jacques Rousseau*, translated by J. and D. Weightman, two vols (London and New York, 1966).

The following are also important: La Chalotais, *Essai d'éducation nationale ou plan d'études pour la jeunesse* (Geneva, 1763); Rolland d'Erceville, *Compte rendu* in *Recueil de plusieurs des ouvrages de Monsieur le Président Rolland* (Paris, 1783); Turgot, *Œuvres* (9 vols, Paris, 1808), vol. VII; and Diderot, *Plan d'une Université Russe* in *Les Œuvres complètes de Diderot* (15 vols, Paris, 1798), vol. III. The tractates by La Chalotais, Turgot and Diderot have been translated with short introductions in F. de la Fontainerie, *French Liberalism and Education in the Eighteenth Century* (New York, 1932), and there is also an annotated translation of La Chalotais' *Essai* by H. R. Clark (London, 1934). Reference should also be made to *La Chalotais éducateur* by J. Delvaille (Paris, 1911). The student of the period immediately preceding the Revolution should consult *Helvétius: his Life and Place in the History of Educational*

Thought by Ian Cumming (London, 1955), and the article on Helvétius and Holbach in *Social and Political Ideas of some Great French Thinkers of the Age of Reason* (ed. Hearnshaw, London, 1930). Some interesting material and an excellent bibliography are to be found in Louis-Grimaud, *Histoire de la liberté d'enseignement en France* (4 vols, Grenoble, 1944), vol. I; and the whole period is well covered in Book VI (vol. II) of G. Compayré, *Histoire critique des doctrines de l'éducation en France* (2 vols, Paris, 1904), in M. Gontard, *L'Enseignement primaire en France, 1789–1833* (Paris, 1959), and in F. Ponteil, *Histoire de l'enseignement en France* (Paris, 1966). The last-named contains a most useful bibliography.

An investigation of the educational ideas which were beginning to ferment in the latter part of the eighteenth century is worth while for its own sake; but another interesting topic is the exact state of education in France at the time when the Revolution broke out. (See Chapter 1.) As has been indicated, there was a tendency at one time to believe that the educational provision in the latter days of the *Ancien Régime* was negligible, and that what did exist was inefficient and moribund. A good deal of research—largely in local areas—has made it evident that this view must be modified. Dr N. Hans has shown that we in England have also tended to underestimate our educational achievement in the eighteenth century.[1] At the same time it cannot be said that any exact agreement has been reached in the case of Revolutionary France. The student who is interested should consult E. Allain, *L'Instruction primaire en France avant la Révolution* (Paris, 1881); A. Babeau's three volumes *La Ville sous l'Ancien Régime* (Paris, 1880), *Le Village sous l'Ancien Régime* (Paris, 1878), and *La Province sous l'Ancien Régime* (Paris, 1894); A. Franklin, *Vie privée d'autrefois—écoles et collèges* (Paris, 1892); and Vallet de Viriville, *Histoire de l'instruction publique* (Paris, 1849)—especially

[1] See *New Trends in Education in the Eighteenth Century* (London, 1951).

the tables on p. 276. See also the statistical monographs written by L. Maggiolo and listed in A. Silvy, *Essai d'une bibliographie historique de l'enseignement secondaire et supérieure en France avant la Révolution* (Paris, 1892); refer to the Index. In A. F. Villemain's Report to the King, submitted in 1843, there is a complete analysis of the statistics relating to secondary education just before the Revolution, and this is compared with the provision in 1842. Villemain was at the time Minister of Public Instruction, and the Report (the exact title of which is rather too long to quote) was published in Paris in 1844. It is an official document and as such carries considerable weight.

Many of the *cahiers* (as was pointed out in Chapter 4) contain references to education. The subject may be followed up in E. Allain, *Le Question d'enseignement en 1789 d'après les cahiers* (Paris, 1886); or more fully in *Cahiers des senechausées et baillages*. For the meaning of the terms *senechausées* and *baillages* see J. M. Thompson, *The French Revolution* (Oxford, 1944), pp. 6 ff. This book gives an excellent short account of the Revolution, though it says very little about educational matters. For this general history Professor A. B. Cobban's *History of Modern France* (2 vols, London, 1962), vol. I can also be strongly recommended, and the relevant chapters in vol. IX of the *New Cambridge Modern History* (London, 1965) should obviously be consulted. E. and J. Goncourt, *Histoire de la Société française pendant la Révolution* (Paris, 1854), and N. Hampson, *A Social History of the French Revolution* (London, 1963) also provide some interesting 'background' material. The *Dictionnaire de la Révolution française* by F. Boursin and A. Challamel (Paris, 1893) is a very useful work of reference.

When we come to the period of the Revolution itself it is more difficult than ever to make a selection among the vast amount of material available. The chief original sources have fortunately been reprinted and are easily accessible. In the very valuable and extensive *Collection des documents inédits sur l'histoire de France* there are seven volumes edited by J. Guillaume and devoted to the minutes of the Committees of Public Instruction which were set up by the Legislative Assembly and the Convention. The first volume is entitled *Procès-verbaux du Comité d'Instruction Publique de l'Assemblée législative* (Paris, 1889). Between 30 October 1791 and 22 August 1792 the Education Committee of this Assembly held 107 meetings. The minutes of these are fully reported in Guillaume's book, which is also furnished with an introduction, appendices and a very full and useful index. Between 1891 and 1907 the same editor issued six volumes dealing with the Convention—*Procès-verbaux du Comité d'Instruction Publique de la Convention Nationale* (6 vols, Paris, 1891–1907). The Committee, which was appointed in October 1792, held 515 séances between that month and the October of 1795. Here again the minutes and other relevant documents are reproduced, and each volume contains a helpful introduction together with notes. There is unfortunately no detailed index to the whole six volumes, but each of them includes a summary of the business transacted at the particular meetings reported. Guillaume is also responsible for a *Note sur L'Instruction Publique de 1789–1808, suivie de Catalogue des documents origineux existants au Musée Pédagogique et relatifs à l'histoire de l'instruction publique en France durant cette période* (Paris, 1888); and he wrote a most informative article on the Convention for F. Buisson's *Dictionnaire de pédagogie* (2 vols, Paris, 1888), I, 520–71. It quotes very extensively from original documents. One may perhaps add that the *Collection des documents inédits* (see above) also includes two volumes dealing with *Procès-verbaux de la Commission Temporaire des Arts—Septembre 1793–Décembre 1795* (ed. L. Tuetey, Paris, 1912–17). These are relevant to the educational history of the period. Another contemporary source of information is the *Moniteur* with its reports and comments on the debates in the Assemblies. The issues of this periodical were reprinted in Paris in 1850 under the title *Réimpression de l'ancien Moniteur (Mai 1789–Novembre 1799)*.

For the text of speeches and reports made to the *Comités d'Instruction Publique* of the Legislative Assembly and the Convention one can consult C. Hippeau, *L'Instruction publique en France pendant la Révolution* (2 vols., Paris, 1881–3). Volume I contains the reports and projects made by Mirabeau, Talleyrand, Condorcet, Lanthenas, Romme, Lepelletier, Calès, Lakanal, Daunou and Fourcroy; so that the whole period is well covered. Volume II deals with 'débats législatifs'. Condorcet's *Rapport et projet de décret sur l'organisation générale de l'instruction publique* is included in his *Œuvres* (ed. Arago, 12 vols, Paris, 1847–9), VII, 469–573. This is translated in F. de la Fontainerie's *French Liberalism and Education in the Eighteenth Century*. There is a monograph on *Condorcet* by F. Vial (Paris, 1902), and one on *Turgot* by Léon Say (Paris, 1904).

A unique collection of original sources is afforded by what are known as the Fortescue Tracts. G. K. Fortescue was Keeper of Printed Books in the British Museum from 1899 to 1912; and in 1899 (when he was still Assistant Keeper) he compiled a *List of the Contents of the three Collections of Books, Pamphlets and Journals in the British Museum relating to the French Revolution.*[1] These collections comprise no less than 48,579 books and other documents dealing with all sides of social and economic life, and with administrative matters. They include also political pamphlets and satires, and a wealth of miscellaneous information. The three collections are classified under the reference-letters FR, R and F; and the following references are of particular interest to the educationist:

FR 231–235	Instruction publique.
R 364–370	Éducation (by years 1785–1829).
R 371	Écoles primaires, 1792–99.
R 372	Écoles centrales, 1795–1800.
R 373	Écoles militaires, 1789–98.

[1] In the catalogue they appear under the heading '*London*, III, 598'.

R 374   L'Université.
R 375   Sourds et muets, 1790–97.
R 376   Enseignement des langues.
R 597   Éducation.
F 493–502   Éducation.

It may be added that J. M. Thompson compiled *French Revolution Documents* (Oxford, 1933), and there is a *Documentary Survey of the French Revolution* by J. H. Stewart (New York, 1951). In the Museum of the Institut Pédagogique National at Paris there are photographic reproductions of the following original documents:

Rapport sur l'instruction publique (Talleyrand) H.E. 11. 144. *Projet d'éducation du peuple français* (Lakanal) H.E. 11. 144. *Rapport et projet du décret sur l'organisation génerale de l'instruction publique* (Condorcet) H.E. 11.1 38. *Projet d'éducation du peuple français* (Lakanal) H.E. 11. 230. *Création et organisation de l'Université Impériale* H.E. 6. 953.

The educational legislation of the period under review is included in such collections as A. de Beauchamp (ed.), *Recueil des lois et règlements sur l'enseignement supérieur* (5 vols, Paris, 1880–98); J. Duvergier (ed.), *Collection complète des lois, décrets et ordonnances...depuis 1788* (4 vols, Paris, 1890); and O. Gréard, *La Législation de l'instruction primaire*, (3 vols, Paris, 1889–1902), vol. I, 1789–1833.

There exists a large number of local studies of educational history in various parts of France. Many of them deal specifically with the period of the Revolution, or they include it. Here again it would be difficult to compile anything like a complete list of these monographs, and almost as difficult to make an adequate selection. But it may be well to mention some of these studies which deal with the *école centrale*. This, after all, is one of the most interesting institutions of the Revolutionary period, although—as has been said—its immediate success was far less than its

17   257   BEA

ultimate importance. It would seem strange, therefore, that there is apparently no detailed and authoritative book on this subject. But when it is written it will be greatly indebted to the pieces of local research on individual *écoles centrales* which are already available. Good examples are B. Bois, *La Vie scolaire en Anjou, 1789–1799* (Angers, 1928), chaps. iv-vi and Épilogue; L. Bourilly, *L'École centrale du département de Var* (Paris, 1903); E. Cheylud, *L'École centrale du département de Cantal* (Paris, 1904); M. Daries, *L'École centrale de la Manche* (Paris, 1923); A. Gain, *L'École centrale de la Marthe à Nancy* (Nancy, 1922); F. N. Nicollet, *Notice historique sur l'école centrale de Gap* (Gap, 1892), *L'École centrale du département des Bouches du Rhône* (Aix, 1913), and *L'École centrale du département des Hautes Alpes* (Aix, 1892); G. H. Quignon, *L'École centrale de l'Oise* (Beauvais, 1913); A. Troux, *L'École centrale du Doubs à Besançon* (Paris, 1926). The subsequent influence of the *école centrale* is touched upon *passim* in C. Falcucci, *L'Humanisme dans l'enseignement secondaire au XIXième siècle* (Paris, 1939); and the second section of F. Vial, *Trois siècles d'histoire de l'enseignement secondaire* (Paris, 1936) also treats of the *écoles centrales*. It is probably the best short account of them that is available.

The institutions of higher education established by, or associated with, the Revolution are dealt with in G. Pinet, *L'Histoire de l'École Polytechnique* (Paris, 1887), in A. Fourcy, *Histoire de l'École Polytechnique* (Paris, 1827), and in F. B. Artz, *The Development of Technical Education in France, 1500–1850* (Cambridge, Mass., 1966). The abortive attempt at training teachers is treated in R. M. Dupuy, *L'École Normale* (Paris, 1884) and in the centenary handbook *L'École Normale, 1795–1895* (Paris, 1896). Among other works dealing with the *écoles spéciales* may be mentioned A. Chuquet, *École de Mars* (Paris, 1899) and E. H. Langlois, *Souvenirs de l'École de Mars* (Rouen, 1836); A. Laussedat, *La Conservatoire des Arts et Métiers* (Paris, 1861), and *Conservatoire Nationale des Arts et Métiers, Recueil des Lois, etc.* (Paris,

1889). See also V. Haüy, *Essai sur l'éducation des aveugles* (Paris, 1786) and Abbé de L'Épée, *Veritable manière d'instruire les sourds-muets* (Paris, 1784).

It remains to mention some of the works which treat more broadly of education during the Revolutionary period. The subject is of course dealt with in greater or less detail in any general history of French education—e.g. Théry, Compayré, Durkheim or Ponteil; but the following treatises are devoted more specifically to this topic and can be recommended to anyone who looks for a fairly comprehensive, but not too detailed, account of it: E. Allain, *L'Œuvre scolaire de la Révolution* (Paris, 1891); M. Gontard, *L'Enseignement primaire en France, 1789–1833* (Paris, 1959); A. Duruy, *L'Instruction publique et la Révolution* (Paris, 1882). The second volume of Louis-Grimaud, *Histoire de la liberté d'enseignement en France* (see above) is devoted to the Revolution; and the first volume of L. Liard, *L'Enseignement supérieur en France, 1789–1893* (Paris, 1882–94) deals with the state of the Universities in 1789 and with higher education during the Revolution. It contains some very interesting *pièces justificatives*. A. Sicard, *L'Education morale et civique avant et pendant la Révolution* (Paris, 1884) forms a useful supplement to the above-mentioned works.

Index

festivals, national, 115–18, 132, 143–4
festomanie, 117
Feuillants, 80
Fichte, J. G., 243, 244
finance, educational, 2, 41, 59, 63, 97, 172, 186, 202, 208, 226
Fontanes, L. M. de, 223
Fortescue, G. K., 256–7
Fouché, J., 108
Fourcroy, A. F., 123, 130, 138, 139, 140, 150, 185, 204, 208–9
Fourier, F. M. C., 226
Fourier, St Pierre, 6
François I, 13
Franklin, Benjamin, 183, 237, 239
Frayssinous, D. A. L., 225
Frederick the Great, 241
free places (*bourses*), 9, 72, 91, 109, 172, 175, 188, 212, 220; see also *Élèves de la Patrie*
French, teaching of, 33, 65, 127, 130, 168, 212

Gambetta, L., 228
'general grammar', 189, 193–4
Genlis, Mme de, 100, 235 n.
geography, 26, 50, 127, 159
German, 50, 104
Germany, 240–4; *see also* Prussia
girls, education of, *see* women and girls, education of
Girondins, 80, 101, 110
Godwin, William, 235
grammar, 26, 49, 51
'Grand Master' (University), 217, 218, 223, 224
gratuitous education, 41, 58, 70–1, 107
Greek, 9, 26, 64, 193, 241–2
Grégoire, H., 122, 129, 159
guilds, 130, 158, 164

Guillaume, J., 102, 255
Guizot, F.P.G., 95, 225, 226, 236
Guyton de Morveau, 138, 140, 147, 160
Gymnasium, 242

Hassenfratz, J. H., 117–18, 140
Haüy, V., 164
Hegel, G. W. F., 243
Helvétius, C. A., 20–1, 28, 231, 234
Henri IV, 1, 16
Herbart, J. F., 23
higher and professional education, 74, 76–7, 87–90, 136–63, 175–7, 206–8, 211
Hippeau, C., 238, 256
history, 11, 26, 52, 127, 194
holidays, 48, 196
Holland, 245
Huguenots, 215
Humboldt, W. von, 243, 244
hygiene, 42–3, 46, 47–8
Hymne à l'Être Suprême, 146
Hymne au Salpêtre 140

illiteracy, 7–8
independent schools, 70–1, 83, 114, 129, 168, 173–4, 180–4, 220, 226, 229
individual teaching method, 3, 6
inspection, 25, 46, 113, 114, 129, 131, 154, 181, 202
Institut National, 76, 102, 176–8, 211
institutes (Condorcet), 87–9; (Napoleon), 220
instituteurs, 103, 128–9
intermediate schools, 195
Italian, 49

Jacobins, 80, 101, 111, 118, 137
Jansenism, 17, 26
Jardin des Plantes, 14, 151–2
Jefferson, T., 239–40

INDEX

For EU product safety concerns, contact us at Calle de José Abascal, 56–1°,
28003 Madrid, Spain or eugpsr@cambridge.org.

www.ingramcontent.com/pod-product-compliance
Ingram Content Group UK Ltd.
Pitfield, Milton Keynes, MK11 3LW, UK
UKHW012330130625
459647UK00009B/179